NAN LYONS

RED ROCK PRESS

New York, New York

ISBN: 9781933176-33-8

Red Rock Press
New York, New York

www.redrockpress.com

Design by Dawn Sokol and Susan Smilanic (Studio 21 Design & Advertising)
Cover by Paul Tunis
Cover 3D Powered by AZUNA(tm). Patent #7,130,126
Index by Sayre Van Young

Lyons, Nan.
  Around the world in eighty meals / Nan Lyons.
     p. cm.
  ISBN 978-1-933176-33-8
  1. Gastronomy. 2. Dinners and dining. 3. International cooking. 4.
Food habits--Cross-cultural studies. I. Title.
  TX631.L96 2010
  641.01'3--dc22
                              2010024118

Printed in Hong Kong

For Ivan, who was with me every mile of the way

—N.L.

~The Journey of~
PHILEAS FOGG

A SYNOPSIS

Around the World in Eighty Days by Jules Verne was first published in French in 1873, and appeared later that year in English.

Mr. Phileas Fogg, "an enigmatic gentleman," according to his creator, regularly dines and plays whist at the Reform Club in London.

On October 2, 1872, Phileas and fellow club members talk about a recent robbery. One member suggests that the world is so large a thief might hide easily and never come to justice. Fogg objects, claiming that a man could make it around the world in 80 days exactly. This sparks a

debate, settled with a gentleman's wager: £20,000 if Phileas Fogg can circumnavigate the globe in 80 days. Putting his entire fortune at risk, Fogg confidently accepts the challenge, and sets out that instant. To win his bet, Phileas Fogg must be back in the Reform Club at quarter to nine on the evening of December 21, 1872.

En route, Phileas collects his manservant, Jean Passepartout. The pair leaves London at 8:45 p.m. on a train heading to Dover. At Dover, they take a ferry across the English Channel to Calais where they catch a train to Paris then switch to another

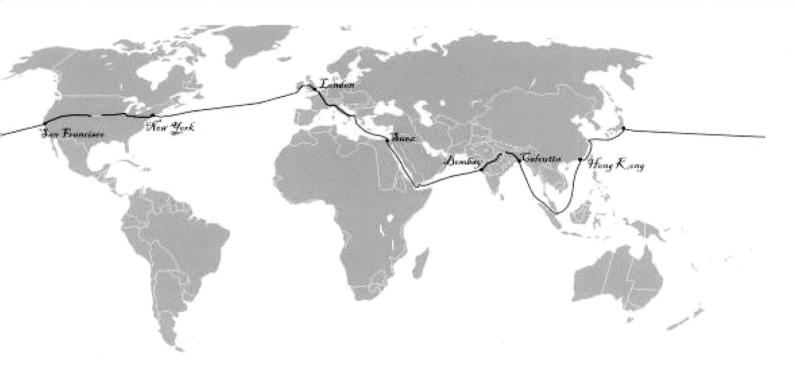

train to Italy. Travel proceeds without difficulty to the steamship Mongolia, routed to pass through the Suez Canal to the Red Sea, then cross the Indian Ocean to Bombay.

Day 8, the ship briefly stops in Suez and takes on some dangerous supercargo, one Detective Fix from Scotland Yard. Due to Fogg's abrupt departure from London, Fix considers Fogg the prime suspect in the recent bank robbery. The detective aims to arrest Fogg, and his strategy is to slow down the ship to give the warrant from London time meet him in India.

The ship docks in Bombay on Day 19. Fogg and his valet board a train headed to Calcutta. But in central India, the train halts—there are 50 miles of missing track! Undaunted, Fogg buys two elephants and hires a local guide to manage the gap.

While on their elephants, Fogg and Passepartout witness a funeral procession. Their guide explains the beautiful young widow is to be sacrificed on the pyre of her deceased husband against her will in a local tradition called a *suttee*. Fogg decides to rescue Aouda. Under Fogg's direction, Passepartout impersonates Aouda's dead husband and jumps from the lit pyre causing the mourners to flee in terror. On Day 23, the elephants bearing the men, and now Aouda, arrive in Allahabad, and board a train, reaching Calcutta the next day.

Fogg's company barely catches the noon steamer bound for the British colony of Hong Kong. The Rangoon stops for half a day in Singapore. Here Phileas and Aouda find a moment to enjoy a carriage ride.

The Rangoon arrives in Hong Kong on Day 36. To slow Fogg, Fix gets Passepartout (who has the tickets for the next ship) drunk. In a stupor, Passepartout barely makes the ship, only to discover that he inadvertently has stranded his master and Aouda in Hong Kong. Passepartout jumps ship at the next port.

Meanwhile, Fogg finds a pilot boat to take him and his lady to Shanghai to catch the S.S. General Grant on its way to the U.S. Passepartout catches up, and the Fogg trio, still followed by Fix, sets out on the three week voyage across the Pacific, arriving in San Francisco on Day 62.

Fogg and friends, and his follower board a train headed east, but the Sioux ambush them and capture Passepartout. Fogg leads the U.S. cavalry to save his man before catching a train to Chicago where they transfer to one bound for New York.

In New York, they've just missed the last ship to Liverpool. Time running out, they board a steamer going to France. Once afloat, Fogg uses cold cash to buy the ship from the captain and change course. It's full steam ahead. Fogg reckons he'll be back in London on Day 80.

However, when our traveler disembarks, Fix pounces, arresting him on British soil. The police hold Phileas Fogg overnight.

In the morning they discover the real robber had entered police custody three days earlier, and Fogg is set free. Too late—he has lost his wager. Though it is not all for nothing, he asks lovely Aouda to marry him. She accepts, and Fogg sends Passepartout to fetch a reverend. En route, Passepartout realizes it is *not* December 22, it's December 21.

Fogg's calculations failed to account for crossing the International Date Line. The valet rushes back to his boss with this stunning news. Phileas Fogg sprints to the Reform Club where the clock reads 8:44 with seconds to spare, and he is victorious.

—*Paul Tunis*
Editor

~ CONTENTS ~

~ CARTE OF RECIPES ~

The Journey of
Nan Lyons

PHILEAS FOGG WAS NOTHING BUT PRECISE when he gave himself 80 days or "1,920 hours or 115,200 minutes" to circumnavigate the globe.

Had Fogg not been so dedicated to the ticking of his pocket watch, he might have built into his dizzying schedule enough time in stopovers to actually stop over for a dining experience or two. Even Marco Polo, who had his hands full looking for a route to China, took time out to smell the noodles. You might say that Jules Verne missed a delicious opportunity by not having Phileas Fogg go around the world in 80 meals.

Verne, who after all knew Phileas best, tells us that when Fogg dined at the Reform Club, his home away from home in London, it was without particular interest in what reclined upon his plate. Seated at his usual table, no matter the day or the season, Phileas always made the same choices: a plate of fish, a plate of meat, and a plate of pudding for dessert. It was a meal that any self respecting nanny could rely on to mold the palates of her young charges to British culinary perfection. Fogg craved neither fillet of blow fish accompanied by Madagascar cranberries or Cactus Soufflé or even Lavender Saffron Gelato. He was never in danger of being exposed to the joys of fusion confusion.

It might at this point be of some interest to explore the word "meal." The dictionary defines meal as "the act or the time of eating a portion of food to satisfy the appetite." There is, however, no mention of the pleasure, the excitement and the pure joy that can be engendered by a meal that is a truly unforgettable experience.

Anyone who thinks that what is on one's plate is the only factor that translates into a splendid dining experience has never had the thrill of coming upon Chez Hole in the Wall, light years removed from the penetrating gazes of culinary mandarins who roam the earth seeking out the newly-anointed gods of Michelin. Chez Hole could never satisfy the mandarins' quest for the Golden Frisée.

Chez H definitely was created not by a consortium of bankers and film moguls but by the

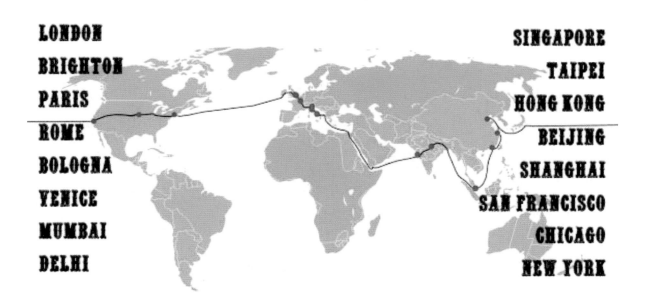

LONDON
BRIGHTON
PARIS
ROME
BOLOGNA
VENICE
MUMBAI
DELHI

SINGAPORE
TAIPEI
HONG KONG
BEIJING
SHANGHAI
SAN FRANCISCO
CHICAGO
NEW YORK

poor souls who tirelessly run it. One of them is usually the chef-owner, who wears his heart on his tomato spattered sleeve. Most important, it was not created to serve the world's most bizarre new recipes made from creatures more at home on the pages of a sci-fi novel than in a kitchen.

Before boarding my own gastronomic express and revisiting some of my more toothsome destinations, I think it only fair to warn you, though I'm writing this in the first person delicious, I feel no need to dissect a menu with the ferocity of Hannibal Lecter or discuss, at unbearable length, the single herb that made my pork chop unforgettable.

Since I have always been an equal opportunity traveler, I feel compelled to ask: What good is an unforgettable meal at an unforgettable restaurant if you can't sleep it off at an unforgettable hotel? Or, what might be of special interest in the restaurant's milieu, to provoke a bit of exploring? I've always found that no matter how superb a restaurant might be, the memory will be that much sweeter if accessorized with a *soupçon* of information about the surrounding area.

In keeping with the spirit of adventure that propelled Phileas Fogg on his journey, I've expanded his itinerary somewhat, to include a few succulent detours that would accommodate my favorite exploits. It's true that my travels, unlike Fogg's, usually focus on food, both humble and haute, and so, *Around the World in Eighty Meals* is meant to be an oral history, in the most personal sense of the word.

—*Nan Lyons*
New York City

London
—The Journey Begins

"Gentlemen, I'm on my way."

– Phileas Fogg to his Reform Club friends

WHEN PHILEAS MADE THAT SOMEWHAT obvious statement at Charing Cross Station, his fellow club members took it with a grain of pessimism, since Fogg, they agreed, was clearly doomed to lose his bet. Had they really heard Phileas correctly, earlier at the club, when he assured them that he would go around the world in only 80 days? Indeed. It must have been something that Fogg had eaten for dinner that caused this dyspeptic fantasy. They might have been on to something since the menu at the Reform Club, in the 1800s, was filled with choices that could hardly pass for spa cuisine. Not to mention that most of the food was overcooked, over sauced and overrated. More to the point, in London, a gentleman's club depended on its stodgy British classics, albeit done with a French accent, to keep the membership happily renewing their memberships.

DINNER WITH FOGG

Jules Verne doesn't name the actual dishes that Fogg tucked into on that auspicious late-afternoon but since we have a club menu of the era, courtesy of The Reform Club itself, it's not too difficult to imagine what Fogg, one of the world's least adventurous eaters, would have chosen.

He might have started with *Consommé de Volaille a la Royale* (chicken broth). He probably wouldn't have gone with the *Potage Crécy* (puree of carrots, chicken stock and cream) because Phileas might have thought it too rich right before a lively game of cards.

His fish course would depend on what he ate earlier (late morning) at the club. Verne did note it was broiled in a [Worcestershire-like] Reading sauce but doesn't name the fish. If I had a vote, I would have ordered the *Blanchailles* (small whitebait, a fish found in the Thames, usually sautéed or fried and served with a mustard sauce). True, fried foods are as indigestible as cream soups but knowing Phileas as well as I do by now, you can bet that he had the trout that afternoon.

Now, for the meat or game entrée, Fogg might have felt that even he would forgo the beef trolley for a plate of *Cotelettes de Mouton à la Reforme*, (lamb chops), a specialty of the club, accompanied by artichokes done in the English fashion (which meant steamed to a dreary beige). Finally, for dessert, *De La Pryme Pudding*, an extravagant citrus confection that added several pounds, or in this case stones, by just its mention. The pudding could very well have been the cause of Phileas' delusion, as his friends must have characterized his travel plans. To end his dinner, Fogg would have ordered a savory, as was usual. In this case, he might have chosen the Parmesan Toasts, just to add an Italian note to his meal.

After such a grand repast what can anyone say except *Bon Appetit*!

London's reputation for food at the time that Phileas Fogg lived his intriguingly eccentric, not to mention precise, life was even worse than its reputation for child labor. Roast beef was not only served with Yorkshire pudding but with its own social security card. Since the days that Fogg dined with such relish at the Reform Club even he would have to agree that the level of cuisine in his beloved city has been upgraded.

Today, instead of fish and chips, you're likely to find poached eggs in puff pastry, or baked avocado over vanilla cream. *Nouvelle Cuisine* replaced boiled cabbage and kidney pudding faster than a speeding crumpet. Restaurant openings produce more buzz than the Royal Family. Of course, by now we know

REFORM CLUB.

Samedi, 26 *Mars*, 1870.

PREMIER SERVICE.

Potage Crécy à la Belle Hélène.
Consommé de Volaille à la Royale.

POISSONS.

Truites, sauces troyenne et génevoise.
Blanchailles à la Diable.

ENTRÉES.

Bouchées à la " Vanity Fair."   Côtelettes de Mouton à la Réforme.

RELEVÉS.

Filet de Bœuf à la Renaissance.

SECOND SERVICE.

Salade à la Romaine.

RÔT.

Canetons rôtis au Cresson.   Artichauts à l'Anglaise.

ENTREMETS.

Pouding à la De la Pryme.*   Gelée à la Carthaginoise.

RELEVÉS DE RÔTS.

Parfait au Citron.   Paillettes au Parmesan.
Dessert et Fruits.

Courtesy of The Reform Club

Reform Club Menu from 1870

that the venerable lady with all the diamond hair ornaments is happiest with clear consommé and orange juice in front of the "telly." She is no longer a culinary reflection of her subjects. There's no doubt about it, London has gone from barely edible cooking in the 19th century to one of the more renowned, adventurous culinary capitals in the 21st.

Visiting London today means never having to say you're hungry. Because of its dynamic and ever changing food scene, Londoners collect restaurants the way that Camilla collects princes. Chefs-in-waiting from all over Europe and Asia vie for a chance to simmer in some of London's most coveted kitchens. There is even a shiny new name for the ever evolving traditional English menu to give it a nationalistic spin: "Modern British Cuisine."

In the past, the British may have been accused of having under performing taste buds, but the folks who have brought us Shakespeare, Mick Jagger and David Beckham were also among the first to discover that Auguste Escoffier could wield a mean sauté pan. More than a century before Marco Pierre White tasted his first snail and Gordon Ramsey humiliated his first sous-chef, and even before Jamie Oliver did his first striptease, Escoffier was the toast of London. The new French cuisine he introduced made the British forget all that nonsense with Napoleon. Escoffier is credited with originating the very first hotel dining room in London. Before that, well-brought up people regarded eating in public as something that only the great unwashed indulged in. No one with any breeding would be caught dead chewing a chop in full view. Escoffier, with his sumptuous menu and opulent setting in the Savoy Hotel, made dining out not only acceptable but the height of fashion.

My own restaurant recollections in London have been slightly more eclectic then Escoffier might have approved of, and through the years they've run the gamut from a battered truck serving take-out at a flea market to some of the more captivating restaurants in the city.

A FOOD VAN NAMED "DESIRE" – #1

The van that I speak of was devoted to fast food at the Bermondsey Antiques Market (also called the New Caledonian Market) in London. Even though Bermondsey was once in jeopardy of being replaced by a housing development, for the moment the threat has passed. I can only hope that it and that remarkable food van will be just where I left them the last time I was in London. If not, they will survive just as vividly, in my memory.

The scuffed, almost-white food van (that I fondly call "Desire") was the only place at Bermondsey to get something to keep the bitter chill of the dawn hours from hastening the onset of osteoarthritis. Of course, that was a known risk for the flea market junkies who regularly showed up there at a very frigid 6 a.m. The only beacon of hope at that hour was the lorry's *carte du jour*, which was limited to fried bacon sandwiches on slabs of white bread accompanied by thick mugs of dangerously hot tea, the memory of which still brings tears to my eyes. The drill was always the same. People lined up as soon as they arrived so that they could fortify themselves for the cold, damp treasure hunt that lay ahead. The van's "chef" could be counted on to look out on his crowd of shivering devotees with a benevolent smile, no matter the weather and no matter how many burn scars from the hot bacon fat he exhibited like badges of honor.

The available choices at the lorry might strike you as one step away from prison food. However the excellence of the bacon or the sausages served almost anywhere in England, even at a flea market, elevates a British breakfast, no matter how humble, to a near religious experience.

Without a doubt, if Phileas Fogg had a proper English breakfast today his meal would include a perfectly brewed pot of Earl Grey, thick slices of fried Irish Bacon, several small, fat, crisply browned sausages known as bangers, a mound of fried potatoes, toast made from perfectly-buttered, crustless white bread (orange marmalade and honey on the side, of course) and a small broiled tomato half just for the hell of it.

As for me, I could eat breakfast three times

a day in London, and look forward to each comforting feast. But, back at Bermondsey, by no stretch of the imagination could you have referred to the bacon sandwiches and scalding tea as a proper British breakfast. Still, at 6 a.m. in the freezing dawn, they fed an incredibly pleasurable addiction. Those bacon sandwiches are, to this day, one of the best meals I've ever had in London.

THE SAVOY GRILL – #2

Ivan (my husband and writing partner) and I had saved for months just for the privilege of dining at the Savoy Grill on our first trip to London. Aside from its reputation as the embodiment of all that was elegantly upper class in hotel dining, it was also the restaurant on whose rug Winston Churchill had flicked so many of his cigar ashes.

Unfortunately, the first sign of trouble arose when the waiter brought the menu and we found, to our horror, it was entirely in French. The only French that we were familiar with at the time was French toast and French fries, neither of which happened to be on the menu. We decided to tough it out and make low mumbling noises that sounded faintly foreign and, if all else failed, point randomly but with some authority to listed suggestions. The waiter, who quite possibly had served crowned heads of state and members of parliament, was not in the mood to be charmed by the obvious discomfort of two upstarts from the New World. In a voice that would have frozen liquid nitrogen he asked, "Does Madam know that she has ordered, as an hors d'oeuvre to accompany her martini, a veal chop?"

In the years that followed our first, but far from last, social disgrace we began to realize that dining out in a renowned restaurant didn't have to be preceded by obtaining a prescription for Valium. And it was not an opportunity to examine one's self worth. The truth is, if you really get down to the basics, no matter the restaurant, you are only renting space at a table for a short duration, and buying the food that

Joint of Beef on a Pewter Dish *by George Smith*

continued on page 22

THE SAVOY GRILL'S MILIEU

Even though The Strand, the long boulevard that runs from Trafalgar Square to Aldwych, is a wonderful walk lined with churches, theaters and shops, of late the bloom is definitely off its rose. It has become commercialized, filled with budget restaurants and is just a bit grubby at the edges. When it comes to the Savoy Grill's milieu, nothing can quite compare with the Savoy itself. The glitzy Art Deco chrome and glass entrance to the Savoy Hotel has always looked as if, at any moment, Fred and Ginger might come twirling out the door, but the hotel's history is even more glamourous.

The glamour started after Richard D'Oyly Carte opened a small theater in the Strand, showcasing new Gilbert and Sullivan operettas. He was desperate to make his theater more popular with people from outside of London. In those days, sleeping overnight in town was usually done at a friend's home. Only the rabble stayed at public places such as inns and coach stops. Enter César Ritz, a young hotelier from the Riviera, and Auguste Escoffier, his even younger chef. D'Oyly Carte hired them to establish a large, multi-storied lodging of the finest quality so that English society would finally find it acceptable to have a sleepover. Voila!! A grand hotel was born.

the restaurant happens to be pushing that day. So the next time that you feel as if you're attending a job interview, conducted by the waiter, you can be certain that you're in the wrong restaurant.

The original chef at the Savoy was a really hard act to follow. Auguste Escoffier opened the room in 1899 and from the very first was considered no mere flash in the pan. If he were around today, one can only imagine his shock at the new streamlined choices added to the Savoy's menu. It's been gently nudged into the present with a lighter, British Modern touch. To everyone's great

relief, no coronets have been bent out of shape in the process.

The Savoy Grill had one foot in the 1890s and another in the 1920s when it was the darling of London's jazzy flapper set. Remarkably, The Grill still displays its stylish versatility in its ability to deal with 21st century culinary modes.

In the past, most of The Grill's specialties leaned heavily toward a perfect dinner menu for Mary Poppins. There was an impressive roast beef trolley manned by an expert carver, Steak and Kidney Pudding, Oysters with Cumberland

Sausage, Boiled Bacon, Braised Turbot and everyone's old favorite, Pease Pudding (a thick mass of split peas cooked down to the consistency of industrial glue).

However, the Savoy waiters always made a festive ceremony at tableside when they served their famous Sherry Trifle. Sir Winston, who was usually no one to be trifled with, was so impressed that he returned, time after time, to table number four after a hard day in parliament.

Today, as I write about the Savoy, I know that what I remember with such fondness is almost sure to change, and for the better. The hotel has been closed for more than a year, Grill and all,

undergoing a major renovation. My spies tell me that when the Hotel re-opens it will surely be as glamourous and historic as ever. Great pains have been taken to restore the Savoy to its original opulence in even the smallest detail. The new Grill Room will be overseen by The Gordon Ramsey Group and so the menu may have a few of Gordon's brilliant additions but old favorites will be in residence, roast beef trolley and all.

THE SAVOY GRILL/ THE STRAND/
   TEL: 0207-836-4343
Expensive

RULES – #3

Years before, when Gordon Ramsey was just a gleam in Michelin's eye, there I was, sitting on a velvet banquet, sipping a glass of champagne and wondering if it was gastronomically, as well as socially, correct to spoon paté directly into my mouth, without help from its accompanying toast points. It was the beginning of my love affair with Rules.

Sad to say, the Rules of today has become a restaurant for rather lukewarm consideration, not

only by the food critics but also by theatergoers who need a convenient Covent Garden address for dining. Over the years Rules has been almost forgotten by London's smart set as well as by most guidebooks. It's regarded as little more than a footnote or worse, a safe place to find "Continental cuisine"—the culinary kiss of death. Few people still think of Rules as a genuine Dickens-era treasure, where Thackeray dined and Charles himself would show up for a plate of kippers in the best of times. Rules is a Maiden Lane institution that has stubbornly hung on for over 200 years. Long may it sauté!

The plush, ruby red banquets were the first things that I noticed as I was led to my table. They seemed to glow against the cream colored walls. Soft light filtered into the room through a stained glass ceiling and illuminated the tables. My first visit to Rules was in the '60s when members of parliament used to show up regularly. I might have been just a bit late as a pacesetter, since Rules first opened its door in 1798. Through the years, the color of the walls has melted into a mellow Victorian sepia like a faded photograph. Rules was and is its own time warp, with a menu to match.

As for some of their dishes of yesteryear, you can always count on Steak and Kidney Pie; Spotted Dick (stop snickering), a spongy custard made with suet and dried fruit; and the ever popular, Treacle Pudding. When game is in season, Rules can play it as well as the best of them to produce a rare venison steak.

The most fun for me is throwing my latest cholesterol report to the winds and ordering the extravagant cheese course after dessert, of course. Usually, a whole round of Stilton the size of Pittsburgh is rolled to the table so that you may cut yourself an extravagant wedge. Add a glass of Port, and Dickens would really be proud.

RULES/35 MAIDEN LANE/ TEL: 020-7379-0258
Moderate

RULES' MILIEU

Since you're just a scone's throw from Covent Garden and London's theater district, Rules has a handy, secret exit that will make getting there a snap. If you ask someone from the restaurant, he'll show you the tiny tunnel, opposite its front door. Even though the tunnel looks like the kind of place Jack the Ripper loved to ply his trade, the courageous will find it opens up opposite the Savoy Hotel, right on the Strand. If you continue on the Strand it's a short walk to Covent Garden. The area around Eliza Doolittle's old haunts has been transformed from a vegetable market into a trendy delight filled with shops of every description and enough casual dining choices to keep even Henry Higgins quiet. The Garden is at its most colorful on the weekend when there are street performers and a small crafts market.

THE IVY – #4

If ever a restaurant had the theater to thank for its glowing reputation, it would be The Ivy. A beloved haven for thirsty Ophelias and hungry Hamlets, The Ivy has been the Sardi's of London ever since it hung out its sign in 1911. The *mise en scene* that plays out on a daily basis makes it the perfect hangout for the star-struck as well as the stars. There are more neck-craners at The Ivy than you'll find in a flamingo park.

"Who's that in the corner?"

"Who just left to change before the curtain?"

Careful, the answers might ruin The Ivy's favorite guessing games. Adding even more drama to the surroundings is the steady hum of the latest backstage gossip. Some say that the ghost of Noel Coward haunts the place but if that's true, I'll bet even he has trouble getting a table; the room is always SRO.

As for the ambiance, what becomes a legend most? In this

case a clubby room, more steak house than theater joint, with butter-soft, green leather banquettes and harlequin colored stained glass. There's a great collection of contemporary art on the walls to ogle, that is if you get tired of ogling the famous faces in the crowd. All of this can be done while tucking into The Ivy's heaping platters of British soul food such as bangers (sausages) and mash (mashed potatoes drizzled with onion gravy), Bubble and Squeak (a mound of mashed potatoes and cabbage) and a classic Shepherd's Pie that would bring a tear to the eye of any self respecting sheep. I advise you to go for the gold when it comes to desserts. They're pure nursery, the kind that would make any nanny's heart beat faster. But beware, they're definitely off limits for those who failed their last stress test. Among the most dangerous are Custard Bread Pudding and the Butterscotch Tart.

THE IVY/ 1-5 WEST STREET/ TEL: 020-7836-4751
Moderate

 THE IVY'S MILIEU

As I've said, The Ivy is just a short walk to Covent Garden, which explains why the theater crowd finds it so appealing. But if you can bear to leave "Theatreland," as the Brits call the streets that surround The Ivy, take a turn along Charing Cross Road, and you'll be well rewarded. There you'll find an irresistible browse in Foyles, one of the world's most exciting book stores. The sheer enormity of its collection as well as the wonderfully rumpled look of the place will instantly turn any butterfly back into a bookworm. It was opened in 1903 by the Foyle brothers and in this age of the dreaded mega book chain, is still family owned. Eat your heart out, Barnes & Noble. Amongst the nearly seven miles of books, you can find all the latest page-turners, but if you happen to be wearing your overalls you can dig way back into the stacks and probably come up with a first edition of the Dead Sea Scrolls. At Foyles, anything is possible.

FOYLES/ 113-119 CHARING CROSS ROAD/ TEL: 020-7434-1574

 # The Ivy's Shepherd's Pie

- *2 ⅔ pounds good-quality minced [chopped] lamb and beef (mixed, and not too fatty)*
- *Salt and pepper*
- *Vegetable oil for frying*
- *2 cups onions, peeled and finely chopped*
- *2 cups sliced button mushrooms*
- *2 cloves garlic, crushed*
- *3 tablespoons thyme, chopped finely*
- *½ (scant) cup flour*
- *¼ cup tomato purée*
- *33 ounces dark meat stock*
- *¼ cup Worcestershire sauce*
- *¾ cup red wine*

For the mashed potato
- *8 large potatoes*
- *Salted butter*
- *Heavy cream*
- *Salt and pepper*

SERVES 6

Season [with salt and pepper] the meat mixture. Heat some vegetable oil in a frying pan until it is very hot and cook the meat in small quantities for a few minutes, then drain in a colander to remove all the fat. In a heavy pan, heat some more vegetable oil and gently fry the onion, garlic and thyme until they are very soft. Add the meat, dust it with flour and add the tomato purée. Cook for a few minutes, stirring constantly. Slowly add the red wine, Worcestershire sauce and dark meat stock, bring it to the boil and simmer for 30–40 minutes. Strain off about 1 cup of the sauce to serve with the pie. Continue to simmer the meat until the liquid has almost evaporated. Take it off the heat, check the seasoning and allow it to cool. Preheat the oven to 400° F.

Peel and cut the potatoes into even-sized pieces. Cook them in boiling, salted water, drain them and then return to the pan over the heat to remove any excess moisture. Using an old-fashioned hand masher or a mixing machine or a potato ricer, purée the potatoes and mix them with plenty of good butter, a little cream and season with salt and pepper to taste.

To make the pie, put the meat into a large serving dish or individual dishes and top with mashed potato. Bake for 35–40 minutes.

BOROUGH MARKET – #5

For a fascinating look at a gastronomic bazaar, I always head to Borough Market, the ultimate experience in open air noshing.

The original Borough Market started out in medieval London as a place for farmers and merchants to eat, meet and make deals. It was located atop London Bridge, that is, before it fell down (the bridge, now a supersized souvenir, resides in Arizona). The market was so popular that it grew and grew, spilling out onto the streets around the bridge. As a nod to progress, in 1276 it was moved to a larger outdoor site. It wasn't until five centuries later, in 1754 that a new market was opened on Southwark Street, a short walk from the Thames.

Today, Borough Market sprawls over more than four acres, all of them choc-a-bloc with enticing edibles. The panorama of meats, fish, picture-perfect fruits and veggies, not to mention other gourmet goodies, is enough to make a grown chef weep. In fact, you can see them at Borough all the time, perhaps not crying but definitely buying. The best restaurant kitchens in London have crates from Borough Market filled with everything from olives to ostrich.

Brindisa's Chorizo Iberico

Photo by Ewan Munro

With its aromatic sausage shops, its arrays of cheeses from around the planet, its wine merchants, its fragrant pastry shops and tapas stands, Borough Market is Graze Central. Londoners stroll among the stalls picking up a salmon croquette here, and a glass of mulled wine there, loving every minute of it, as I do. My personal favorite requires standing on the line that forms in front of Brindisa's chorizo stall at

continued on page 31

BOROUGH MARKET'S MILIEU

Since you'll be in Bridget Jones *territory (the film was shot nearby) you might want to roam some of the old streets around the market. Of course, the whole area is changing, and a distressing attack from "The Boutique People" is all too imminent. Until then, for a taste of Elizabethan London you've only to walk over to the awe inspiring reproduction of Shakespeare's Globe Theater, and spend some quality time in the House of William.*

Although the Globe is only open on a limited basis (May through October) for the Bard's biggest hits, it's open year round for tours of the museum. I was so moved by the dedication that went into the meticulous restoration, I was actually teary. It is truly miraculous in its authenticity. Since the new Globe was built even more information has been uncovered (literally) about Mr. S.

Archeologists believe they have found the ruins of yet another theater that Will both acted in and wrote for. The Globe museum will have more up to date information if you care to visit.

Another intriguing relic of London's past is to be found on Clink Street, famous for its jail, now a mini museum. It goes without saying that the phrase, "thrown into the clink" has something to do with all of this. The jail has become a favorite tourist attraction. You can have the dubious pleasure of being thrown into the clink yourself since short visits for tourists can be arranged.

GLOBE THEATER/ 21 NEW GLOBE WALK/ BANKSIDE, SOUTHWARK/ TEL: 020-7902-1400
CLINK PRISON/ 1 CLINK STREET.

noon for one of its spicy sandwiches. The cooks char the sausage over glowing coals and the resulting aroma accounts for the long queue, not to mention my ongoing dedication. The rules for chorizo chomping at Brindisa's state that its fabulous sandwiches are only available until 2 p.m. sharp—but not to worry. If you arrive, God forbid, at 2:01 you can be sure of an almost limitless display of other yummies to sample as you browse the endless aisles at the Borough.

Borough Market/8 Southwark Street/ Southbank/ Tel: 020-7407-1002

THE RIVER CAFÉ – #6

Despite the fact that its name seduces you into believing that your reservation will produce a table with a stunning view of the Thames, the inside of The River Café is, without a doubt, landlocked, at least from any of its floor-to-ceiling windows. But take heart, come spring and summer, when the café's tables overflow out into its idyllic garden, you can actually catch a glimpse of its namesake. It's comforting to know that there is still some truth in advertising. However, location, location, location, as it applies to The River Café, that darling of London's smart set, is not a dream come true. Its address, as it has been for over 20 years, is a block from the ends of the earth, or to be more specific, it's in the Borough of Hammersmith.

Housed in an old olive oil warehouse since 1987, The River Café was designed by Britain's

Courtesy of The River Café

most distinguished architect Richard Rogers (not the one who wrote *South Pacific*). Rogers counts among his other monumental achievements The Pompidou Centre in Paris and London's Millennium Dome. What made this giant from

Courtesy of The River Café

the world of architecture decide to design an Italian restaurant way out in the boonies? That's a no-brainer—he's married to the chef and co-founder of The River Café, Ruth Rogers. The other founder Rose Gray, who sadly died in February of 2010, was usually right beside her overseeing operations as Ruth stirred up one of her voluptuous marinara sauces.

From the day they opened The River Cafe, Ruth and Rose agreed on a menu that was focused on the freshest food of the season, no matter that it often translated into prices that resembled sums on Warren Buffet's annual report.

Assuming that you've made a reservation at least a month in advance and can find The River Café, you will be rewarded by experiencing the highly personal style of an extraordinary restaurant. The proof of the *panna cotta* is written in its Michelin stars, actually one star that it has

continued on page 34

THE RIVER CAFÉ'S MILIEU

For the most part, the London Borough of Hammersmith is off the beaten track when it comes to major tourism. Not many travelers take time to explore this gritty part of the city. Not to worry, the Hammersmith tube stop makes getting there from central London, an absolute cinch. The problem is, if you've arrived a bit early for your reservation at The River Café, what to do? Nearby is The Dove, a teeny, tiny pub, dating back to the 17th century. It's rumored that Nell Gwynne and Charles II were regulars. Even more fun is the fact the Guinness Book of Records lists The Dove as the smallest bar in Britain. Claustrophobics take note. Neuroses aside, The Dove, with its cozy fireplace and intimate atmosphere is perfect for an aperitif or some after dinner lingering.

The Dove/19 Upper Mall/ Hammersmith/ Tel: 020-8748-9474

Courtesy of The River Café

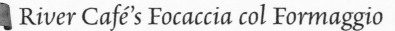 

River Café's Focaccia col Formaggio

- 2¾ cups bread flour
- 1-plus tablespoons sea salt
- 3 tablespoons extra virgin olive oil (Ligurian is ideal)
- 1 cup grated or thinly-sliced Stracchino cheese [see NOTE]

Note: *Stracchino is a slightly acidic, cream cheese native to Lombardy. If you cannot find, you might substitute Mascarpone.*

SERVES 12

Place a large mixing bowl in a warm place and sift the flour into it. Add 1 tablespoon of sea salt and 3 tablespoons of olive oil. Stir in ¾ cup of warm water with a wooden spoon and mix together until you have a sticky dough, then cover with a cloth and leave in a warm place for 30 minutes.

Tip the dough onto a generously floured work surface. Coat your hands with flour and knead it for several minutes until it becomes smooth and elastic. Divide the dough into two, place in separate bowls, cover both with cling-film and leave for 15 minutes.

Preheat the oven to 425° F. Flour the surface again and roll out the first ball as thinly as possible into a 16-inch diameter disc. Lightly oil a flat baking tray or pizza pan and lay the dough down on it carefully. Grate or thinly slice the cheese over the dough so that it covers the surface within ⅓ inch of the edge. Scatter with sea salt.

Roll out the second ball of dough to the same size. Place it on top of the first one to cover the cheese, and press it down lightly at the edges. Drizzle the surface with olive oil, scatter with sea salt and place in the oven for 25 minutes, or until the crust is light brown. Cut the flatbread into wedges while still warm.

held since 1989. Despite the fact that the café is often filled with notables and knights of the realm, mere mortals are as well taken care of as Prince Harry's girlfriends. When I leave after a visit, and trudge back to the tube stop, there's always a broad smile on my face, as well as a smear of sauce Bolognese on my cuff.

Since my last visit, The River Café has gone through a major trauma that led to the extensive renovation of its *haute moderne* interior. In the spring of 2008 the café suffered a horrific fire. Its open grill (a familiar part of the restaurant's décor) exploded and sent flames shooting up to the ceiling. The River Café closed to lick its wounds and redesign its grill. To insure that the catastrophe would be turned into a positive omen, the owners and their chefs made a pilgrimage to Italy to stoke their own fires and renew their menu. The River Café, somewhat remodeled, but not at the expense of its original clean, bright, elegant design, rose from its ashes and reopened the following fall. I'm told that the only really new element is a dramatic white wood-burning oven that is the restaurant's flaming centerpiece.

My favorite table at the café is the one closest to its extravagantly long bar. It stretches out, as if it were a stage, to present platters of irresistible hor d'oeuvres and sinful desserts. As I obsess over the glories to come, I always relax with a glass of chilled Prosecco served over a fresh peach, the house drink.

But the real action at the River Café is centered around the oven that turns out chicken and duck, as crisp as parchment, glazed roasted veggies and perfectly moist fish. The rest of the menu, since it changes not only seasonally but weekly and sometimes twice daily, makes recommending specialties a bit too risky. In truth, everything at The River Café is special. There's also the fact that since the renovation, the café has added new triumphs to the menu that I can only imagine (a trip back, sooner rather than later, for research purposes of course, is definitely required). Whatever the changes, the one thing that is almost always on the dessert menu is Chocolate Nemesis. True to its forbidding name it's as addictive as any narcotic on the market. Don't hesitate!

THE RIVER CAFÉ/ THAMES WHARF STUDIOS/ RAINVILLE ROAD/ HAMMERSMITH/ TEL: 020-7386-4200
Soooo Expensive!

TEA AT BROWN'S HOTEL – #7

I've had tea all over London but I keep coming back to Brown's. And I don't mean for just a cup of tea, I mean Tea, with a capital Tantalizing.

Brown's was born back in the 1800s, sparked by, as the song goes, an impossible dream. And that impossible dream belonged to Lord Byron's valet, James Brown. Brown thought if he could make Lord Byron comfortable (no small task) then he could do the same for the rest of London. The hotel has had a few re-furbs along the way to spiff it up a bit, but essentially it's the same Brown's where Eleanor and Franklin (the Rs) spent their honeymoon, and where the writing desk that Rudyard Kipling used during his stays remains tucked into a corner of its library.

Whenever I've had a hard day picking Piccadilly clean, I know that I can park my shopping bags, sink down into one of Brown's ultra soft sofas and have what seems to me one of the more extravagant teas in town, and I do mean the works: first, tiny delicate sandwiches filled with cucumber or smoked salmon or sardine paste, then warm scones, dripping with butter and clotted cream, and then to end this sensuous fantasy, Lilliputian fruit tarts glistening with caramelized jam. If there's still room for just a bite of something, then perhaps a thick slice of raisin loaf topped off with freshly whipped cream. Best of all, though by my last sip of Tea, I'm in danger of a sudden attack of insulin shock, I can savor the memories of sugar plums dancing in my head.

Courtesy of Brown's Hotel

BROWN'S HOTEL/ 30-34 ALBEMARLE STREET/
  TEL: 20-7493-6020
Moderate

BROWN'S MILIEU

You're so close to Fortnum & Mason, that venerable holder of the coveted royal warrant: Purveyor to the Queen, why not pick up a jar or two of the Fortnum label orange marmalade. It's one of her favorites. Who knows when you'll have another opportunity? It's at 181 Piccadilly.

Brown's Hotel's Scones

For the scones
- 4½ cups plain flour
- 5 tablespoons baking powder
- ½ cup sugar
- ¼ teaspoon salt
- 7 tablespoons diced butter
- 1 cup milk
- ½ cup (heaping) sultanas (golden raisins)

For the eggs wash
- 2 egg yolks
- 2 teaspoons milk
- Pinch of sugar

For serving
- Clotted cream
- Strawberry jam

MAKES 20 SCONES

Sift flour, baking powder, sugar and salt into a bowl.

Using your fingertips, rub the butter into the flour until the mixture resembles coarse cornmeal.

Add the sultanas and the milk and mix well. Once it starts to come together, turn out on to a lightly floured surface and knead gently until it forms a smooth, soft dough.

Encase it in plastic wrap and chill for one hour.

Roll the dough out on a lightly floured surface to about 1 inch thick and cut into rounds with a 2 inch cutter. Place on a baking tray lined with parchment paper.

For the egg wash, mix ingredients together in a small bowl and brush the tops of the scones twice.

Bake for 10 to 12 minutes until golden brown. Do not over-bake them or they will be dry.

Serve them warm with clotted cream and good strawberry jam.

– recipe by Fabien Ecuvillon, Head Pastry Chef

THE PROSPECT OF WHITBY – #8

What's the very best thing about a visit to a pub in London? Aside from the gazillion choices of stout and draft beer, it would have to be a traditional pub lunch. Of course, if you really need a quick schooner for what "ales" you, you're apt to be more interested in the liquid libations.

Not that all pubs or public houses are historic. Many of the ones found on almost every street corner in London are just run-of-the-mill neighborhood taverns. But, there are others that can go head-to-head with the Tower of London in terms of longevity. In fact, The Prospect of Whitby, which dates back to 1543, makes Buckingham Palace (1702) seem like a new housing development.

Albeit somewhat of a tourist hangout, the Prospect of Whitby also attracts the locals, who admire it just because it's still standing after almost six centuries. When it was first built it was known as "The Devil's Tavern." After it burned to the ground, it was rebuilt and renamed with the help of a good PR agency, The Prospect of Whitby. Today it's billed as the oldest riverside pub in London.

THE PROSPECT OF WHITBY/ 57 WAPPING WALL, TOWER HAMLETS/ TEL: 020-7481-1095
Moderate

THE PROSPECT OF WHITBY'S MILIEU

You're so close to the Tower of London, you might just be hauled off to the block. Drop by anyway, of your own free will, of course. It's delightfully creepy.

London/
Front Burner

AMAYA

Amaya is a totally new concept in Indian restaurants—for London that is. In fact you could call it an Indian tapas bar. Small plates of food arrive, elegantly presented and without the usual starters or mains. Not only is it delightfully non-traditional, it's a real budget saver. But on most nights Amaya is jammed with adoring trendies who don't have to worry about the price of their curries. The specialty of the kitchen is grilling, be it meat, fish or fowl.

AMAYA/ 15 HALKIN ARCADE, MOTCOMB STREET/ TEL: 020-7823-1166

JAMIE'S ITALIAN

He's everywhere, this young British dynamo and everyone seems to adore him. This time Jamie Oliver is speaking with an Italian accent and his *cucina italiana* has stirred up quite a ragu. It's always SRO with pasta hounds who have wallets that are a lot trimmer than their waistlines. Who knows where Jamie will strike next?

JAMIE'S ITALIAN/ 19-23 HIGH STREET/ KINGSTON-UPON-THAMES/ TEL: 020-8912-0110

Brighton/
A Detour

Yes, I know, I know. On his manic schedule, Phileas would never have had the time for a fun trip to another seaside resort as he hurried to Dover to catch the boat train that would carry him *tout de suite* from England to France. But if he had, he would surely have packed an extra carpetbag and headed for Brighton.

Imagine one of the most perfectly preserved Regency settings, with a dash of Coney Island on the side, and you have the very essence of Brighton. Its seafront promenade is bordered by tall, elegant colonnades. Wedged between them are tacky souvenir shops which act as very inelegant punctuation to the magnificent architecture that is synonymous with Brighton. Even the long piers that jut out like fingers into the Atlantic are elaborate; though timeworn. Once, the piers were crowded with amusement park rides and actual crowds strolling from food to game concessions amid a carnival-like

atmosphere. Today the piers are rather rundown shadows of their former selves, but even so, the views are wonderful and the piers offer a compelling vision of the past.

Facing the entire length of its seaside, Brighton's handsome parks, splendid crescents and dignified squares are still beautiful enough to have been chosen as the perfect Edwardian backdrop by Masterpiece Theatre. Thackeray must have had the same thought since he used Brighton as a setting for *Vanity Fair*.

Brighton became popular in the late 18th century as a fashionable seaside resort, a place for Britain's upper classes, to carefully immerse themselves, fully clothed into the ocean. But the tourists of today will soon find out that Brighton is no day at the beach. Instead of soft sand and the expectation of sun, going to the beach means wearing heavy shoes with thick soles to protect tender feet from its sharp stones (the Chamber of Commerce refers to them more charitably as "pebbles"). As for sun, don't count on it. Sun worshippers have been turned into agnostics after a day of gray skies and chill air. Most of the time it's wiser to bring your umbrella than your tanning lotion.

Of all the curlicues and doo-dads that ornament many of the structures in Brighton, nothing quite compares to the ornamentation of The Royal Pavilion. It was built between 1815 and 1852 by the architect John Nash using the vivid imagination of the then Prince Regent, who later became George IV, as his blueprint. The prince was more suited to the life of an interior decorator than that of a future monarch. He lavished all the king's horses and all the king's contractors to make the Royal Pavilion, some say with a bit of a sneer, the eighth wonder of the world.

The façade of the Pavilion is a recreation of an Indian potentate's palace, complete with domes and minarets, while the inside is an opium dream in full flower. Bollywood at its wildest has yet to outdo the prince and his magnificent obsession. The Pavilion walls are covered with miles of hand-painted wallpaper, and the rooms are filled with, rare oriental antiques, countless carved dragons and boatloads of gold leaf. All of this gives real meaning to the phrase, "a king's ransom."

A surprise is that the permanent population in town has a show-biz profile. Since the late 1800s, Brighton has served as a haven for theater folk who, like the Oliviers, preferred to live far from the madding crowd of London. At present, Brighton is again a chic outpost of London, attracting a whole new, young group of weekenders and commuters.

ENGLISH'S SEAFOOD RESTAURANT & OYSTER BAR – #9

If you make an excursion to Brighton for a whiff of sea air, don't leave town without tucking into a platter of Colchester Oysters, laid out in glistening majesty on English's long white marble counter.

Step two is to wash them down with a glass of chilled champagne (English's doesn't require this, but I do).

This venerable Oyster House, a century and a half old, has been owned by the same family since 1945, so they've really gotten the hang of it by now. Yet these are not quite the glory days of yore for English's—recent comments indicate that the management has become too casual. Still, the outstanding oysters as well as English's history make a stop here appealing. Originally the site of three fisherman's cottages built over 400 years ago and located in the oldest part of Brighton, English's is as much a part of the landscape here as the sea.

The oysters may be from Colchester, a town in Essex County renowned for its bivalve beauties, but English's clientele comes from all over the British Isles and beyond. Fish fanciers have included Dame Judy Dench, Jeremy Irons, Tony Blair and Ewan McGregor. Years ago Charlie Chaplin was a regular as was Sir Laurence and Joan Plowright, his wife. They've all enjoyed English's denizens of the deep but, unfortunately, not at the same table.

When I visited, English's took its Dover Sole so seriously that the waiter leaned forward and in hushed tones asked, "On the bone or off the bone, Madam?" When was the last time that anyone asked you that question except, perhaps, your orthopedic surgeon?

ENGLISH'S SEAFOOD RESTAURANT & OYSTER BAR/ 29-31 EAST STREET/ TEL: 127-332-7980
Moderate

ENGLISH'S MILIEU

If Brighton is famous for its restorative sea breezes, the one thing that it can't cure is tchotchke fever, a malady best treated with a flexible credit card and a pair of comfortable shoes. The section of Brighton known as the Lanes is a collector's dream or a custom's inspector's nightmare. It's made up of a maze of tiny streets, some so narrow that single file is a must. The locals call them "twittens," and they're lined with shops that were once fishermen's huts. The somewhat quirky merchandise one may find in them runs the gamut from antique crystal chandeliers to mugs with Princes Di's picture. Kitsch is the name of the game although there are tiny curio shops that have a treasure or two. The twittens weave in and out like the alleys of a Moroccan bazaar, and by the time you find your way back, you may be weaving a bit too. Even if you're not into clutter, the Lanes are a unique shopping experience, and one I always find great fun.

~ FRANCE ~

Paris

"Arrived Paris Thursday 3 October, 7:20 a.m.–
Left Paris Thursday, 8:40 a.m."

—Phileas Fogg's notebook

PHILEAS KNEW THAT HE HAD ONLY the briefest of time after arriving at the railway station in Paris to transfer to the train that would take him and his dedicated sidekick Passepartout on to Italy. Clearly no time for a fragrant *café au lait*, no time for a buttery *brioche* topped with jam, no time to read *Le Figaro at* a sidewalk café. Phileas even ignored endless opportunities for *un petit déjeuner* "to go" as he hurried along. But for me, leaving Paris without a nibble of croissant, a bite of quiche or a quick drink at the Ritz would be unthinkable.

This is a city to be savored slowly.

Whether it sizzles or drizzles, whether it's springtime or fall, Paris is an original. Even more original than any of its *haute couture* or *haute cuisine* creations, or the radical concepts and ideas of its philosophers, Paris stands by itself as the keeper of the flame of excellence present in almost every aspect of French life. It's no wonder that the French think of Paris as the most perfect city. Some might say that, if anything, this is an understatement.

Most people who come to Paris come

to have an affair—the affair is with the city itself. It can be seductive and irritating, captivating and rude, exciting and confounding. Much of the time, exasperating! Paris has all of the qualities necessary for a really successful *affaire du coeur*. Perhaps, most maddening of all, the city makes you work really hard to receive a few crumbs from its endless banquet of delights.

As I found out somewhat painfully on my first visit, your average Parisian can be as prickly as a porcupine, as sharp as a jalapeño and as rigid as my mother-in-law. Speak with the locals and it's always the best of times and the worst of times all sautéed into one. But then, as if by magic as you sit at a sidewalk café sipping an *apéritif*, that same porcupine morphs into Maurice Chevalier. *C'est la vie en Paris*.

Perhaps the *raison d'etre* for all of this has something to do with that little dustup better known as the French Revolution. You remember: the one that led to the use of severed heads to decorate the Place de la Concorde. Even today the motto, *Liberté, Égalité, Fraternité,* signifies to the French their complete rejection of anything that encroaches on their independence, and that includes the pesky hordes of tourists who think that once they've bought their plane ticket, they own the place. Parisians' way of dealing with this constant invasion of their city is to operate blithely in their own sphere of awareness and entitlement. To the rest of the world they may seem cold and even arrogant at times but in reality they just need to set themselves apart in order to preserve the very way of life that makes them Parisians.

Paris continues to be on the best of terms, not only with its glorious past but also with its vibrant present. Daring 20th-century structures such as the Pompidou Center and I. M. Pei's glass pyramids at the Louvre sprout up among the Beaux-Arts beauties that once dominated the Paris skyline.

As for other past treasures, the royal relics and monuments to all those guys named Louis have been spruced and regilded, old parks remain pruned to perfection and even the Eiffel Tower which was always illuminated has been made to twinkle after dark, somewhat like a Christmas Tree. (I'm not completely thrilled about that.) Although it hardly seems possible, Paris has never looked more beautiful.

The last time I saw Paris (sorry, I just couldn't resist) the ever present obsession with food and the perfection of the dining experience was second only to sex in making a Parisian's heart beat faster. In fact, I'm not really sure that food was second. Politics, ambition, fashion and even the economy all take a back seat to dinner at a three-star Michelin marvel. You can almost hear the *La Marseillaise* in the background every time Michelin hands down one of its sparklers.

Today, fabulous restaurants throughout the world have begun to dim the exclusive pilot light of French *haute cuisine*. Still, the French take little notice of culinary achievements outside their borders and continue to revel in their gastronomic heritage. For the Parisian, a "remembrance of things past" would have more to do with the details at a great meal than anything Proust wrote about, including his beloved madeleines.

Nowadays, a great meal in Paris doesn't necessarily mean revisiting the scene of the shrine. But in the past, first time travelers to Paris usually spoke of La Tour d'Argent or Tallievent or Maxim's in reverent tones, as if they were to be visited like museums or landmarks. In truth they are, like the Three Musketeers, immortal. Far be it for me to suggest that Tallievent ever be taken with a grain of *sel*, since it is to this day revered as one of the hautest of the *haute*. In the words of Arthur Miller, "attention must be paid." As for Tour d'Argent, I could spend a whole afternoon there with only an espresso and a window table (though almost impossible to obtain) from which to worship the view of Notre Dame.

Maxim's, on the other hand, has to be approached with a bit more caution. The beauty of its decor tends to blur the fact that Americans are sometimes treated with even less respect than the Germans were during the Occupation. There is rumored to be an infamous section set aside in the front of the restaurant, where French is almost never spoken. It's known by the staff as "the American Zoo." However, should you be successful in breaking through the barricades and escaping into the main room, you will be rewarded with one of the more seductive restaurants in all of Paris.

MAXIM'S – #10

There is just no way to overlook this temple to Art Nouveau opulence as you pass by. That famous sign, with its mischievous, topsy turvy lettering seems to alert the world that entering will lead to nothing but pleasure. Who of a certain age can forget Maurice Chevalier's naughty smile as he sang, "I'm Going to Maxim's?" Both the song and the place stood for the kind of turn-of-the-19th century gaiety that made Paris so exciting and provocative. Through the years, Maxim's has become a monument to the Belle Époque period; an extraordinary example of Art Nouveau style at its most sensuous.

All mahogany swirls and curves, gilded flourishes and floral extravaganzas etched into its multicolored stained glass, Maxim's décor evokes an iconic pre-World War I Paris in all its heady flamboyance. Today, everyone still seems to be going to Maxim's but unlike Chevalier and his endless search for wine, women and song, they come for the souvenirs, postcards and the *prix fixe* menu. If the gods should smile upon them, then perhaps a table in the main room will be grudgingly awarded under that impossibly gorgeous, stained-glass ceiling.

Who was Maxim, anyway? For starters, Maxim's was opened by Maxime (with an 'e') Gaillard who had worked as a scruffy waiter in a scruffy bar in the late 1800s. Fed up with watching the scruffy clientele nod off over their absinthes, he decided to expand into the world of *haute société*. In 1893, with the help of friends, he opened a slightly risqué café dedicated to

the white-tie-and-tails set. It was a place where *messieurs* could come without their *femmes*. Instead, they brought an ever changing cast of dazzling *mademoiselles* to waltz the nights away. All well and good for Maxime, but sadly, hanky panky doesn't always keep the champagne flowing. He was finally forced to put his little bistro on the market. Maxime was rescued by Eugene Cornuché, who had money and the vision to make Maxim's into a Belle Époque showstopper. More than a century later, Maxim's permitted *Gigi* to be filmed there as an homage to its gloriously checkered past.

Today, Maxim's is more a state of mind, a fantasy from the past rather than a gourmet's dream come true. That's not to say that it's impossible to have a good meal, but instead of seeing Michelin stars you're more likely to see a plate of passable bistro cuisine dressed up by its surroundings and wearing a *haute couture* price tag. Long gone are the days when foie gras and oysters graced every table. And the only time that you may come upon a real, live Parisian is on a Friday evening. It's still a bit of a tradition on Friday for the regulars, that is those who are left, to take to the dance floor during dinner. Poignantly, the orchestra that played the waltzes Chevalier made famous, has been replaced by one lonely pianist . . . enough said!

While it's true that you're more likely to be seated next to a computer programmer than a Greek shipping magnate, to overlook Maxim's is to overlook a fabulous chapter in the history of Paris.

MAXIM'S/ 3 RUE ROYAL/ TEL: 01-42-65-27-94
Very Expensive

MAXIM'S MILIEU

You don't have to go very far to find the perfect place to visit after dinner at Maxim's; you just have to climb the flight of stairs next to the coat room. When you reach the second floor, you'll find an even more stunning Art Nouveau refuge. As rare as Parisians are downstairs at Maxim's, they crowd the upstairs Imperial Bar for pre-theater drinks and post-theater sustenance. Chanel, St. Laurent and Lagerfeld are the flags most saluted here. All in all, the upstairs crowd is one of the most soignée in the city. Ivan and I stumbled on this hidden gem of a room when celebrating an anniversary. We ordered a bottle of champagne with dinner and the waiter, sensing the occasion, asked if we wanted to finish it upstairs, to Maximize (pun definitely intended here) our romantic interlude.

When you finally emerge from Maxim's, the Rue Royale is literally at your feet. It runs from the Place de la Concorde to La Madeleine. Needless to say that the street is dotted with some of the most elegant shops in tout-Paris. Christofle, Villeroy & Boch, as well as the toothsome Fauchon are all ready to lighten your Euro load.

LES DEUX MAGOTS – #11

To go from *un grand luxe* of a landmark on the Right Bank to a fabled Left Bank hangout that has attracted some of the more important minds of the last century, one has only to walk across a small bridge, Le Pont Neuf. But no matter what its size, it's a bridge to the intellectual heart and soul of Paris.

Les Deux Magots is unmistakable. A huge sidewalk café, with wicker bistro chairs overflowing onto much of the sidewalk, it sits at the corner of the Boulevard St. Germain and the Rue de Rennes. Waiters rush from table to table with small carafes of *vin ordinaire* or glasses of Pernod, trying desperately to navigate their cramped terrain. Rain or shine, day or night, the chairs are always occupied at Les Deux Magots.

In the '20s, they were filled with novelists and painters, obsessed with living *la vie de bohème*. Hemingway and Fitzgerald were two renowned faces in that crowd. Much later in the '40s and '50s, when Paris was free of its German jailers and it was safe to speak one's mind again, those same bistro chairs again held the intellectual *crème de la crème* of Paris. Sartre, Camus, Genet and Simon de Beauvoir all did much of their philosophizing over their cafés filtres at Les Deux Magots. Existentialism was as much a part of the menu

as eggs *en cocotte*. There they sat, hour after hour, filling ashtrays by the dozen as they debated their radical positions on love, life, death and where to buy the best brioche.

The rivalry between Les Deux Magots and the nearby Café de Flore is long lasting. Regulars alternated between the two but Deux Magots always seemed to have the edge. It surely did with Hemingway. In *The Sun Also Rises,* Jake Barnes meets Lady Brett at Les Deux Magots. When you think about it, where better could they have met? Everyone else met there.

Deux Magots is named for the statues of two old Chinese men, which have been carved into a wooden pillar inside the café (the term magot, roughly translated means Chinese commercial agent). The statues act as inscrutable overseers to the never ending action below. Seated atop pedestals meant to represent money boxes, their perches seem completely appropriate since Les Deux Magots is an absolute goldmine.

The same sun that Hemingway found so compelling continues to rise over Deux Magots but perhaps without quite as much brilliance as in the past. Nowadays, *le déluge des touristes* have managed to dislodge the literati. If you drop by, as I do whenever I'm in Paris, you'll no longer

find the intellects of the century. The only heated discussions to be heard might have more to do with who gets the next table then who might be the next Camus.

An ideal time to sit outside at Les Deux Magots, or in fact anywhere in Paris, is on a chilly fall day to watch the world stroll by. Add to the near perfect scenery a cup of its superb chocolate accompanied by a pencil thin, buttery *jambon en baguette* and, without a doubt, you'll have one of the better meals in town.

Les Deux Magots/ 6 Pl. St. Germain/ Tel: 45-48-55-25
Inexpensive

LES DEUX MAGOTS MILIEU

The ancient streets that wind around Boulevard St. Germain are among the more fascinating in Paris. They are choc-a-bloc with tiny bookstores, food shops and cafés. It will surely make you crazy if you try to visit them all, no matter how seductive they are. A much better plan is to visit Bon Marché on the rue de Sèvres. Bon Marché opened for business in 1852, and has the distinction of being the oldest department store in the city. Unfortunately, today its prices are definitely 21st century.

Bon Marché charmingly maintains the feeling of an exotic bazaar where you might come upon any number of treasures, especially in its crowded basement. A special bonus comes from simply following your nose. It will lead you to Bon Marché food hall, La Grande Épicerie, right across the street. It's an epicurean paradise, filled, floor to ceiling and counter to counter, with tempting goodies for takeout. Whoever said that bringing a snack back to the hotel would compromise your standing in The Gastronaut's Guild?

Au Bon Marché/ La Grande Epicerie/ 24 Rue de Sèvres

LE PRÉ CATELAN – #12

Nestled in the lush foliage of the Bois de Boulogne, Le Pré Catelan is an exquisite opportunity to celebrate the first day of the rest of your life. No one seems to be immune to its sumptuous Belle Époque backdrop. Think New York's former Tavern on the Green as done by Renoir. It's the perfect place to start an affair and the perfect place to end one. It's also the perfect place to drink a toast to the future, sitting amid the gilded symbols of the past.

Le Pré Catelan has a lot more going for it then its lush interior. In summer or autumn, the terrace spills out onto its flower and herb filled Shakespeare Garden, the kind of setting that might have appealed to very tragic Camille if only cough drops had been invented in time. Shade is provided by a massive beech tree, said to be one of the oldest in Paris.

If the weather or the season is uncooperative, then the magnificent dining room makes up for the loss of its garden setting. Period murals, lush velvet draperies and sparkling crystal chandeliers complete the picture. At least, that's what Pré Catelan looked like the last time I was there. Since it's considered to be a Parisian treasure, I'm sure that any significant changes would require a vote in the National Assembly.

Le Pré Catelan has a very special meaning for me, aside from just a glorious place in which to open my oysters. The first time I set eyes on the lavish dining room it had been thrown into the kind of chaos that only a film crew could cause. The whole room, usually aglow with polished silver and cut glass, was lit by blindingly bright klieg lights and crisscrossed with cables.

Perhaps this was not the ideal day to drop in for lunch, but it was a very singular day for my husband Ivan and me. Just a few years earlier we had written *Someone is Killing the Great Chefs of Europe*, a novel of food, murder and sex. Our thought being that it might resonate not only with normal readers but with foodies, serial killers and sex addicts, as well. Much to our amazement, we turned out to be absolutely right.

We were at Pré Catelan that first time to watch the filming of our book. Now, I know that authors are usually outraged by the horrendously idiotic choices that the trillion people involved with bringing a book to the screen, including the director's cleaning lady, are apt to make. Of course, the narcotic used to dull the author's pain is usually a check with many zeros. Miraculously, in our case, the choices that were made resulted in a film that both Ivan and I were proud of.

It was at Pré Catelan amid all the disorder and general upheaval that we saw the characters from our book come to life. Ivan and I were two sappy kids from New York who saw what we created become better than real: it became magic.

It might appear that affection as well as nostalgia for Pré Catelan has clouded my palate. Not so. I've returned many times since *Great Chefs* was filmed there, and the restaurant's menu is as impressive as ever.

Some time ago, Pré Catelan was bought by Gaston Lenôtre and his wife Colette. Gaston was known as the Mozart of French pastry and frozen confections. Sadly, he has passed away but Colette is keeper of the Lenôtre flame. She has determined that Pré Catelan not be considered just another pretty face. Colette has buffed, polished and refined the menu by bringing in Frederic Anton, a protégé of Joel Robuchon and Alain Ducasse. He's still there accumulating even more Michelin stars

Frederic Anton

LE PRÉ CATELAN'S MILIEU

This time it's as easy as a walk in the park. Since you find yourself in the middle of the Bois de Boulogne why not do a little bucolic exploration? However, if you're really intent on exploring the Bois, it might constitute more than your average after dinner walk. The Bois de Boulogne stretches out for over 22,000 acres. It has lakes, hiking paths, exotic flower gardens and even a racetrack. Napoleon III used to hunt wild boar and wolves there. When he grew tired of using it as his personal playground, he donated it to the people of Paris. Today, the wildest thing you'll find in the Bois is a lost tourist.

for Le Pré Catelan's collection.

Le Pré Catelan/ Rue du Bois de Boulogne/
    Tel: 01-44-14-41-00
Expensive

LE GRAND VÉFOUR – #13

Where else in Paris can you sit on a velvet banquette under a plaque marking the spot of Josephine and Napoleon's first date? It may have been a favorite hotspot but when it had opened a decade earlier, Le Grand Véfour was a small café, abuzz with rumors of big trouble coming. If the Louis du jour didn't watch his éclairs, *la guillotine* was likely to become a reality.

Le Grand Véfour attracted some of the brilliant minds as well as some of the dangerous radicals of the revolutionary day. Danton and his buddies plotted and planned as they split an order of *tête de veau*. Much later, Victor Hugo hatched *Les Miserables* there while reaching for a crust of bread. Much, much later, Colette entertained her gentlemen friends at Véfour; she frequented the establishment when she was well into her eighties. Now *that* was really dangerous.

Down through the years there have been legions of artists, writers and politicians with only slightly lower profiles, who have clinked champagne flutes in Grand Véfour's elegant *Directoire* interior. When I have dinner there, I always ask to sit at Colette's favorite table, hoping against hope that some of her glamour will seep into my psyche. Alas, the only thing that seeps

---

 ## LE GRAND VÉFOUR'S MILIEU

Right across the street, the splendid Tuileries Garden stretches all the way to the Place de la Concorde. The garden would be the perfect place to take your evening promenade.

If, however, the mystique of Le Grand Véfour has left you with a serious case of history overload, what better way to clear a cluttered mind than a visit to a shopping mall? In this case, the mall is part of the Louvre so no one can accuse you of frittering away your precious time in Paris. Le Carrousel du Louvre has its own entrance, apart from the museum under a discreet canopy. If you decide to explore the Louvre's mall, disregard the unfortunate invasion by McDonald's which, to be fair, does serve French fries, and instead browse the bookshops and the boutiques. Of course, there's little chance that you'll come upon the Mona Lisa who resides in the museum wing of the building, and is definitely not for sale.

into my psyche is guilt over that last spoonful of *coeur à la crème*.

Over the last century or two the menu may have changed, but Véfour's immense historical significance remains.. In fact, those in charge of bestowing the coveted "listed" designations in Paris, finally elevated Le Grand Véfour to that well-deserved status.

Today, the ever-changing Parisian restaurant scene is all about movie stars, fashion stars and rock stars but not necessarily the ones from that chubby tire guy. *Mon Dieu,* the man from Michelin in 2008 downgraded the wonders that chef Guy Martin stirs up in the kitchen of Grand Véfour, demoting it to two stars from three.

LE GRAND VÉFOUR/ 17 RUE BEAUJOLAISE/ LOUVRE/ TUILERIES/ TEL: 42-96-56-27
Expensive

LE TRAIN BLEU – #14

Think crowded train station. Threads of smoke billow from the trains as they arrive and depart, lovers are saying goodbye, some for the last time. People are arriving to start new lives. Drama, drama, drama! And there you are, observing it all from one of the huge windows of Le Train Bleu. Could you die?!

The Paris–Lyons rail line modeled this glorious buffet on the legendary train that took many of the Parisian elite to Lyons, and then on to the Riviera for a bit of R & R. Le Train Bleu is no ordinary rest stop designed to serve hurried hungry travelers. Although originated by a

Courtesy of Le Train Bleu

railway, it's one of the more gorgeous restaurants in Paris. People with no travel plans at all come to dine at Le Train Bleu just because of its magnificent Belle Epoque ambience.

The food is strictly Brasserie 101 but, as I recall, the onion soup was comforting and a *salade Niçoise* was fresh and appealing. For dessert the *oeufs á la neige* were nursery perfect. Going much further into the menu might prove a disappointment.

Since it opened in 1901, almost nothing has changed. Aside from the usual art nouveau accoutrements, Le Train Bleu is covered, wall to ceiling, with painted landscapes (41 in all) of locales that the actual train passed through. The scenes are separated by massive gilt frames that enhance their heroic size. Surrounded by all this magnificence, what comes out from the kitchen is really of little importance. It's almost impossible to take your eyes from the setting long enough to care. I went to Le Train Bleu for the first time because I was actually going somewhere, and by train. I've returned many times since, just to make sure that what I remembered wasn't some kind of dyspeptic mirage. In 1972, André Malraux awarded the designation of Historical Monument to Le Train Bleu. He couldn't have made a more perfect choice. It's a showstopper and a half.

LE TRAIN BLEU/ 1ER ETAGE GARE DE LYON/ PLACE LOUIS ARMAND/ TEL: 43-43-97-96 MODERATE

LE TRAIN BLEU'S MILIEU

The Gare de Lyon is a wonderfully European train station, so unlike those we have in the States. It's almost a city in itself. Aside from the trains pulling in and out, within its vast space there are bookstores, shops of every description, cafes and all manner of intriguing places to explore.

Le Train Bleu's Old-Fashioned Preserved Duck Foie Gras

- *2 (one-pound) lobes of foie gras**
- *4 cups of clarified duck fat*
- *1 tablespoon of [preferably] Guérande salt [see NOTE]*
- *2 teaspoons of brandy*
- *8 slices of whole-grain bread*
- *Ground pepper to taste*

In this country, raw foie gras comes packed in vacuum-sealed plastic bags. Keep very cold until ready to remove for use; handle foie gras minimally. Rinse, and use the point of a sharp knife to remove carefully the large veins that run through the center of each lobe, and any green.

NOTE: *Guérande salt is a gray, organic salt from the shores of Brittany, available in gourmet markets. However, another organic (non-iodized) sea salt might be used.*

Serves 4

Season the foie gras with the salt and ground pepper. Add the brandy and refrigerate overnight.

Heat the clarified duck fat to 212°F, allow it to drop to 158°F, and maintain this heat throughout the cooking process. Plunge the lobes of foie gras into this fat and turn them over from time to time, cook for 20 minutes. Remove the lobes and allow them to drain on a rack. Wrap the foie gras in new plastic wrap and give them a cylindrical shape; allow to harden in the refrigerator; remove the wrap from the foie gras.

Place the foie gras in a bowl and cover completely with the clarified fat. Keep in the refrigerator for up to ten days.

Remove the fat around the foie gras and cut it into thick (½-inch) slices, add a little fine Guérande salt and coarse-ground pepper. Serve the toasted whole-grain bread separately.

ANGELINA – #15

A chocoholic's dream or nightmare, depending on what your scale tells you, Angelina has been serving hot chocolate to Parisians since 1906, and that's an awful lot of cocoa. They *must* know how to make a pretty good cup by now. But Angelina has never settled for just good—its gloriously wicked concoction called *Chocolat l'African* that is fabled. Richer than Donald Trump, *l'African* is a thick, dark blend (the recipe is a closely-guarded secret), topped with a cloud of whipped cream. Through the years, the young mademoiselles who have crowded in to have *une tasse de chocolat* have morphed into the elegant grandmothers who are now introducing their grandchildren to this scrumptious ritual. Even Coco Chanel was a

regular. Of course, that may have had a lot to do with her name.

The very gilded and mirrored Angelina has dedicated itself, from the time it opened, to the care and feeding of the ginormous sweet-tooth that has always existed in Paris. There's a pastry shop on almost every block, for heaven's sake.

ANGELINA/ 226 RUE DE RIVOLI/
TEL: 01-42-60-82
Expensive

ANGELINA'S MILIEU
The Rue de Rivoli leads up to Place de la Concorde or down to the Louvre. Both are, of course, incomparable. Take your pick.

BAR HEMINGWAY / RITZ HOTEL – #16

The atmosphere in the Bar Hemingway is heavy with reminders of its illustrious past. The writer it was named for conjures up a vision of hard drinking and even harder living. He found that "a moveable feast" is best washed down with a

couple of single malt scotches. You might say that one of the reasons the lost generation got lost was all the time it spent in the Ritz bar. Aside from Hemingway who, rumor has it, shot off a gun after downing a few (the bullet hole is still in the wall), James Joyce and Graham Greene as well as Sartre were Ritz bar devotees.

The Bar Hemingway with its dark wood, comfortable leather chairs and photographs pays homage to its namesake with more than his name. Its menu features Spanish wines and tapas to celebrate Hemingway's bullfighting days. Colin Field, the barman or, as we say today, with some self-consciousness, "mixologist," was voted the best in the world in 2001. His alcoholic contributions include a Picasso Martini made with a splash of Dubonnet. One can't help but think that Pablo would be abstractly proud.

BAR HEMINGWAY/ RITZ HOTEL/ 15 PLACE VENDÔME/ TEL: 43-16-30-30
Expensive

BAR HEMINGWAY'S MILIEU

Milieu, schmilieu, you're at the Ritz, what more is there to say? If you must, a quick turn around the Place de la Concorde and then back to the Ritz for more billionaire watching.

BERTHILLON – #17

You scream, I scream, we all scream for ice cream, but Berthillon's patrons are really serious about this beloved confection. Just to prove it, the line sometimes stretches almost all the way to London. That may be a tiny exaggeration but there really is a long line, whenever this ice cream icon opens its doors. Its lick-as-you-go—don't expect a table or any of those luxe

A cold and sweet mixed blessing

amenities, such as a place to sit down. However, I guarantee that you'll walk back down the block, cone in hand, with a great big smile on your face. No doubt about it, Berthillon will make you forget that you've ever heard of Ben or Jerry or that other guy with the funny name, Häagen-something.

The reason that Berthillon, a

family owned business, has seen its ice creams rise to the top is that the only ingredients they use are sugar, eggs, heavy cream and fresh fruit. Sounds simple, but then you have to put them all together to achieve their double rich, silky phantasma. Unfortunately, Berthillon has no plans for U.S. distribution in the near future. Sob.

BERTHILLON/ 31 RUE SAINT-LOUIS-EN L'ÎLE / TEL: 43-54-31-61

Inexpensive

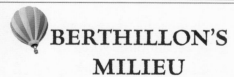 **BERTHILLON'S MILIEU**

The Île Saint Louis is an idyllic place to walk or shop or do anything. Since it's right in the middle of the Seine, the best views of the rest of Paris are all around you. Enjoy them.

Photo by David Monniaux

LE JULES VERNE – #18

Even though I have searched my conscience, there is no way to avoid using a meal that I had at Le Jules Verne as one of my top eighty. Left to my own devices I would not have embraced Le Jules Verne as memorable enough in my personal lexicon of epicurean experiences. But, *mon Dieu*, how can one not include the restaurant named after the literary father of Phileas Fogg, not to mention the *raison d'etre* for my culinary memoir?

In all fairness, I must admit that since I last visited, Le JV has gone through a massive renovation as well as a change of management. Alain Ducasse has taken control, shined up the décor and enhanced this restaurant with its astounding views from atop the Eiffel Tower. Gone are the days when the restaurant relied on its incomparable vistas to make up for its rather pedestrian food. Ducasse excels in making his menus reflect the sensibilities of his restaurants, as well as the people who dine there. Still, even today, one of the best reasons to visit is to gaze out over the City of Light, from atop the most famous landmark in Paris. It gets no better than that.

As for the décor, you would think that any restaurant called Le Jules Verne would have a certain Victorian clubbiness. Not this one. When I was last there it was black, chrome, leather and most of all, nouvelle boring. My spies tell me that it's been redone by M. Ducasse in warmer browns beiges and ambers but still continues to be sleek and spare in style. Perhaps its modern attitude is recognition of the fact that Jules Verne was always ahead of his time.

Le JV may have been regarded as a tourist destination rather than an epicure's dream come true, but by now, my guess is Alain Ducasse has all his bases covered.

Le Jules Verne is reached by a private elevator located inside the southern pillar of the Tower. It whisks you up, more than 400 feet into the clouds, and once the doors open, on a clear day you can see forever.

Le Jules Verne/ South Pillar/ Eiffel
Tower/ Avenue Gustave Eiffel/
Tel: 45-55-61-44
Moderate/Expensive

LE JULES VERNE'S MILIEU

There are, of course, any number of things to do around the Eiffel Tower but they all pale by comparison to the tower. Let's face it; it's been a sight to behold ever since Gustave Eiffel constructed this tinker toy in 1889.

After dinner, don't bother with dessert. Take the elevator that belongs to the tower itself up to the observation deck at the very top, and be prepared to be even more dazzled then you were in the restaurant. The height, measured from the ground to top, is 1,063 feet or the equivalent of 81 stories. Now what dessert could possibly compete with that view of tout-*Paris?*

Paris/
Front Burner

L'ASTRANCE

Located on the rue Beethoven, L'Astrance is a symphony of new menu perceptions. Michelin took note of this when it gave it one twinkler soon after L'Astrance opened its doors. Chef Pascal Barbot continues to amaze his ever growing cult of groupies as well as the rest of his reservations list.

L'ASTRANCE/ 4 RUE BEETHOVEN/
TEL: 40-50-84-40

CHARDENOUX

A perfect recreation of a Belle Époque bistro with a chef/owner who spent years trying to find the ideal place to unpack his soufflé dishes. Now that Cyril Lignac has finally found it, he's whipping up a storm. All the usual suspects are on the menu so tuck into a slice of his paté, and enjoy the scene.

CHARDENOUX/ 1 RUE JULES-VALLÈS/
TEL: 43-71-49-52

~ ITALY ~

Rome, Bologna, Venice/
Detours

As he continued his journey, Phileas made his way by train from Paris to Turin, via Mont Cenis and then on to Brindisi with the accuracy of a guided missile and almost the same speed. It was in Brindisi that he had his rendezvous with the good ship Mongolia that would carry him to Bombay.

Brindisi is not just another pretty port on the Adriatic. It has the distinction of being at the very end of the Appian Way. Brindisi was the point of embarkation for the countless Roman legions heading to Asia with some major conquering plans. Probably, no one was presumptuous enough to tell Fogg that in the year 19 B.C. the poet Virgil mysteriously died in Brindisi, probably in mid rhyme. Or

perhaps, that was the reason that Phileas was so eager to leave.

Actually, it's unlikely that Phileas could have been impressed by any of this time consuming nonsense. Without even stopping for a three cheese pizza or a glass of Chianti he was on his way to India. With the Mongolia ready to set sail, you can be sure that the prospect of Rome-ing around the Eternal City didn't even begin to entice Phileas. Tick-tock, tick-tock.

Personally, there would be no way I could forgo the endless temptations of the *cucina Italiana* or the heady aroma of a rich *salsa di pomodoro* (tomato sauce), simmering in the cafés of the Via Veneto. I know only too well that all roads in Italy lead to Rome.

Rome/
Detour

"We're traveling so fast that everything seems a blur."

—*Passepartout*

Someone once said that most Americans who visit Rome bring with them, packed carefully in their suitcases, their own preconceptions of the city. A very few come with memories of World War II, others with a *Three Coins in the Fountain* romanticism, some arrive with a Hollywood, sword-and-sandal view of the ancient city. All three are possible. Younger first-time visitors have other ideas.

Rome spreads out a banquet of treasures, both new and old to feast upon. The history of the city, much of it ancient, is all around you. Who can resist the urge to fantasize about the Roman version of the Super Bowl, held in the Coliseum, to the delight of a bloodthirsty crowd? Or that vision of Nero, playing his concerto for lunatics as Rome quite literally became the hottest city in the world?

However, in the Rome of today, its formidable history is not the whole story. There is no shortage of cutting edge architecture, as well as sleekly modern restaurants, light years removed from the neighborhood *trattorias* of yesterday. The newer places are crowded with today's versions of Loren and Mastroianni, extravagantly dressed in the latest Fendi, Gucci and Valentino. As for Italian industrial design, it's considered to be some of the most progressive in the world.

Perhaps the truth is that Rome will always be a city within a city. At its very core is the echo of its ancient glory. The 21st century is welcome but only if it agrees to live in harmony with the past.

Rome is called the Eternal City for good reason. Ever since the Romans double parked their chariots in front of the Coliseum, its street life hasn't changed all that much. Rome's ancient monuments are almost side by side with its newest department stores and cinemas. If Caesar were to appear in Rome today, he might be a bit confused by the noise and the traffic but I'll bet he could still find his way to the Forum without having to ask directions. And furthermore, he would be delighted to know that he has added immeasurably to his fame by becoming a really delicious salad.

It's true that Rome wasn't built in a day or a century or a millennium. Modern Rome is one of the great cosmopolitan capitals of Europe. No matter that Milan, its archenemy to the north, believes the Milanese and not the Roman rabble are the ones who invented the last word in sophistication. For the Milanese, that would include money and risotto in that order. but the Romans have learned to thumb their noses at their stodgy compatriots from the north, and continue to excite the rest of the world with their endless zest for life. Romans can survive anything, even the staggering weight of their own history.

The restaurant scene in Rome is almost an embarrassment of riches. It is no exaggeration to say it's possible to stick a pin in a map of the city and come up with an exceptional meal. But even for gastroholics, food is not the only consideration. There are times when atmosphere trumps the tortellini.

Back in the days when I thought that Al Fresco was the name of a used car salesman, outdoor dining was a rarity in the States. Not so in Rome. Dining alfresco is a way of life, not only because of the cooperative climate but also because of the average Roman's dedication to observing and then gossiping about the passing parade. People watching is an art form in Rome, and the *vox populi* is even more popular when you can eavesdrop on it. And let's not forget the glorious scenery just a few feet away. Dining within sight of one of Bernini's bubbling beauties or in an ancient piazza is a common but always major event.

OTELLO ALLA CONCORDIA – #19

A visit to Rome not only means the chance to marvel at the ancient footprint of the city but also to join its residents in living *la dolce vita*. Although it has never led me to take a Fellini-esque dip in the Fontana di Trevi, my visit would certainly include a trip to Gucci, a quick peek into Bulgari and then a chance to linger for most of the evening under the leafy trellises of Otello. This charmer is a near perfect place for savoring the pleasures of relaxed dining while gazing at the moon. Could there be a more perfect culinary experience?

If Dorothy was flabbergasted when she stepped

Trevi Fountain at night

Crowded Spanish Steps of Rome

into Oz, then I can say I felt much the same way when I first entered a narrow stone alley looking for something that resembled a restaurant, and found myself in the courtyard of Otello. The leafy canopy atop the stone walls lets filtered sunlight stream down to highlight its lavish buffet. Platters of heroic proportions are heaped with all the essential elements needed for a really extravagant antipasto.

Otello is not to be confused with some gilded mecca that caters to elite Roman society. On the contrary, it's just a typical neighborhood hangout but in this case the neighborhood is right off the Spanish Steps, some of the most fashionable real estate in Rome. The streets that radiate from the Steps are a shopaholic's dream come true. Elegant boutiques up one side and designer ateliers down the other. The area is one of the top shopping destinations of Rome. And where do you think all those exhausted fashionistas go to stoke up for the next round of fun and Ferragamo? To their cantina of choice—Otello.

At any given lunch or dinner, the stone patio is filled with hungry shoppers and storekeepers who have decided to spend their pre-siesta time grazing on roasted veggies or feasting on Otello's homemade pastas. And then there's always the *tartufo del giorno*, a dangerously caloric dessert of the day. Actually, siesta time is a necessary defense against a possible coronary event. The afternoons that I've spent at Otello are a blur of stuffed shopping bags and stuffed *ravioli*. And they always ended the same way—with a plate of gem-like raspberries buried in freshly whipped cream. *Buona fortuna!*

Otello alla Concordia/ Via Della Croce 81/ Tel: 06-679-1178
Moderate

 OTELLO'S MILIEU

If you've ever seen the film Roman Holiday, *then you remember Audrey Hepburn devouring an ice cream cone as she sat on the Spanish Steps. Romans use the Steps to bask in the sun, to have a quick calzone or to pick up a signorina who looks like a really good sport. For tourists, it's a place to re-group before attacking the shops again. At the foot of the Steps, the Piazza di Spagne, filled with palm trees and flowers, is the real heart of Rome. The Square was famous in the 1800s for the community of artists living along its streets. Keats and Shelly were two of the more renowned members of the group. The house where Keats died has been turned into a Keats - Shelley memorial, (obviously a two poets for the price of one strategy) and is located in the Piazza.*

DAL BOLOGNESE – #20

From the 1700s through the 1820s, the Piazza del Popolo in all its Baroque grandeur was the place to go if one wanted to view a public execution. Festive crowds filled the square, clamoring to see the executioner work his expertise on the

Piazza del Popolo

condemned. At the time, it was regarded by the Romans as fun, Italian-style. Today, my guess is that at Dal Bolognese the only thoughts of public executions are prompted by appearing in the wrong outfit.

When I think of Rome, visions of St. Peter's, the Forum or the Coliseum are not the only ones that come to mind. One of my favorites is sitting out on the terrace at Dal Bolognese in the Piazza del Popolo as the sun goes down. I return to that terrace every so often, to see if Dal Bolognese (DB) is still the Temple of Cool.

DB has long been the place to see and be seen in Rome. A favorite hangout for the up and coming since those who have already come up prefer the anonymity of their corner *trattorias*. But anyone visiting Rome to shoot a film, make

a commercial, do a fashion layout or show off a new lover usually finds the way to Dal Bolognese. And, of course, it never hurts to look like a character out of an Antonioni film.

For all of Dal Bolognese's charisma, its décor is nothing special. Inside you'll find a few cozy rooms for quiet dining but it's the terrace, spilling out onto the Piazza, that is the *in* place to be. The ever present paparazzi hover like a swarm of manic insects to hunt for celebrities. As for the service at DB, the waiter is king. Even being considered for a table on the terrace is dependent on a roll of their very selective dice. No matter that they whizz by without even a glance as you wait patiently in the dim hope of being seated outside. They live by their own code: direct eye contact is never achieved. Don't be daunted, just hold your ground and if you're really fortunate, there will be a sudden cloud burst and magically a table will appear.

In restaurants that thrive on their own celebrity, food can turn out to be just an

afterthought. Not so at Dal Bolognese. The food is always dependable without upstaging the diners. DB is known for the rich sauces and pastas of Bologna. The homemade egg *tagliatelle*, one of the most ordered pastas on the menu, is almost buried beneath a thick sauce Bolognese and a blanket of parmesan cheese. DB's *pièce de résistance* is its heroic Bollito Misto, a dish almost as famous as the restaurant itself. A selection of boiled meats which can include, in varying proportions and combinations, brisket, tongue, duck, chicken, sausage and, for the bravest of the brave, a head of veal (ears and all). The meats recline on a rolling cart called a *carrello*. All of the carving and serving is done with great ceremony as befits a carnivore's dream come true. The sauces served along side are the traditional green sauce made from a combination of herbs and

DAL BOLOGNESE'S MILIEU

It's impossible to resist walking and walking and then walking some more, in Rome—an exquisite Renaissance church here, a majestic fountain there. The most fascinating thing of all is that the names attached to them are familiar to us because of history books, rather than guidebooks. And then suddenly there they are, just waiting to be discovered by you. The Via del Corso, right off the Piazza del Popolo, is lined with impressive Renaissance palaces. The 15th century church of Santa Maria del Popolo is just steps from Dal Bolognese's terrace and is filled with glorious frescos, paintings by Caravaggio, a chapel designed by Raphael, not to mention a few additions by Bernini. Now that's food for the soul.

a *mostarda*, a thick, sweet conserve of seasonal fruits. It may be true that Dal Bolognese is more of a social experience than a dining event, but no matter, it's Rome at its most beguiling.

DAL BOLOGNESE/ PIAZZA DEL POPOLO 2 / TEL: 06-361-1426
Moderate/Expensive

CAFFÉ GRECO – #21

It would seem that visiting the place where Goethe and Lord Byron enjoyed their evening espressos, though not at the same time, would be of more than routine interest. It was for me. The Caffé Greco, which opened its doors for business in 1760, has not only shared two and a half centuries of history with Romans but has served as the favorite coffee house for an impressive list of artists and writers. You might say that Caffé Greco was the beginning of the Age of Starbucks. Over time, the Caffé's regulars have included Casanova, Shelley, Wagner, Berlioz, Liszt and D'Annunzio. One wonders in the case of Casanova when he had the time for a cuppa joe.

Photo by nolitawanders

Although it might have been the clubhouse for the greats and the near greats, Caffé Greco wasn't quite so popular with Pope Leo XII, who in a fit of 19th century pique, or more likely coffee nerves, had the place padlocked. His thought being: less time for schmoozing means more time for praying. Undaunted, the staff handed cups of espresso through the windows to its caffeine deprived fans lined up outside.

It's true that today Caffé Greco has become the kind of tourist magnet that an experienced traveler shuns like the plague but, on the other hand, it's wonderful that this landmark still exists. Bottom line: I, for one, cannot resist its gilded if slightly faded splendor. The lure of the worn burgundy velvet, the shabby paintings on the walls and all that history, for me is irresistible. My favorite spot is the banquette under the portrait of mad King Ludwig of Bavaria.

Caffé Greco/ Via Condotti 86/
  Tel: 06-679-1700
Moderate

IMÀGO / THE HASSLER ROOF – #22

The Hassler Hotel during the '60s was the grandest of the Grand Hotels in Rome, as well as the darling of the Jet Set. Today, the term "jet set" seems so outdated but in those days it conjured up visions of white mink coats and gigolos. The Hassler with its enviable location, at the top of the Spanish Steps, stood like a grand dame, decked out with gilded moldings and brocades. But if you had looked more closely just a few short years ago, you would have noticed that she has a small run in her stocking. That's not to say that the Hassler would ever have been considered a budget hotel. It sported a five-star rating but the spotlight had dimmed a bit, just as it had for the Jet Set.

However, as I said, that's all in the past now that the Hassler has morphed into the Hotel

Photos courtesy of Imàgo

Hassler Villa Medici. It has been buffed and burnished to a fare-thee-well and has regained its gilded reputation. Even though it has been completely refurbed, what remains from the good old days is the Hassler's famous roof restaurant, which has been renamed, Imàgo. While it's true that there are stunning rooftop restaurants at many luxury hotels around town, the Hassler seems to bridge the gap between the glamour of the city's postwar days and the second decade of the new millennium.

The term "brunch" has never been enthusiastically accepted in Rome. I suspect that it has something to do with going to church

continued on page 80

Imàgo's Eggplant Parmigiana Express

- ¼ to ½ cup Peanut oil
- 2 long eggplants
- 6 eggs
- Salt and pepper
- 1¾ cups flour
- 4 tomatoes
- 10 ounces Buffalo mozzarella
- 1¼ cups basil
- 1 cup grated Parmesan cheese

SERVES 6

Preheat oven to 350°F. Warm in the oven enough peanut oil to cover the bottom of a large fry pan. Cut the eggplants into round slices that are around ¾- inch thick and put aside. Whisk eggs along with a pinch of salt in one bowl, and place the flour in another bowl. Then place the eggplant slices in the bowl of flour, and then in the bowl with the whisked eggs, and then once more back in the flour so that both sides are well covered. Then place them once more in the egg mixture and immediately fry in heated peanut oil.

Place the fried eggplant slices on absorbent kitchen paper and salt them on both sides. On the side, cut each tomato into four slices and remove seeds and fleshy inside parts, and then cut the mozzarella into slices.

Prepare fake sandwiches using the fried eggplant discs instead of bread. On each eggplant slice place a layer of tomato, then a layer of mozzarella and then some basil leaves on top, dusting between each layer with grated Parmesan cheese.

Place in the oven for about 7 to 8 minutes, or until the mozzarella melts slightly, then serve.

—recipe by chef Francesco Apreda

for an 11 o'clock mass on Sunday morning. Or perhaps it's just that Romans are not eager to give the impression that they would think of booking a table before noon. They leave that to the Americans. And so, it's much more politic to have Sunday *lunch* at the Imàgo.

In truth, almost everyone still calls Imàgo the Hassler Roof. No matter what it's called, lunch there on the weekend is almost viewed as a ritual. And come to think of it, "viewed" is the operative word. From the Hassler's luxurious rooftop terrace, the panoramic views take in the dome of St. Peters and the Vatican. The Seven Hills of Rome are spread out as far as the eye can see. When people tire of being mesmerized by the scenic wonders, they can feast on Imàgo's perfectly moist frittatas, its tender *tagliatelle*, not to mention its silken *cannoli*, stuffed with mascarpone. For those who just prefer a Campari at sunset, as I do, it's a special delight to watch the purple sky become illuminated by the lights of Rome.

Imàgo/The Hassler- Villa Medici Roof/ Piazza Trinita dei Monti 6/ Tel: 06-699-34726
Moderate/Expensive

HOTEL HASSLER'S MILIEU

Just steps away from the Hassler, the Borghese Gardens are in perpetual bloom. Laid out in formal English style, they seem to go on for miles. The Gardens are not just a place to commune with nature; they're filled with majestic villas that house extraordinary art collections. The largest is the Villa Borghese, whose collection includes Titian, Raphael and Caravaggio. The Villa Julia which was originally the summer home of Pope Julius III has a collection of Etruscan antiquities. Last but not least, the Villa Medici is now the French Academy of the Arts.

BABINGTON'S TEA ROOMS – #23

I know what you're thinking, Babington's really doesn't sound like an Italian name. Right you are—it's not. It's the veddy proper surname of Anna Maria Babington who opened her veddy English enterprise 1893. You could say that Babington's Tea Rooms are steeped in history.

Anna Maria had her work cut out for her since most Italians thought tea was a letter of the alphabet rather than a drink. Linguini with clam sauce was much more common than tea and scones on Italian menus. Miss Babington, stiff upper lip and all, took matters into her own hands. She was determined to provide a homey atmosphere for her fellow Brits to relax in, a place just right for sipping a soothing cup of Earl Grey.

The best reason to stop in at Babington's, after running up and down the Spanish Steps nearby, is that unlike the rest of Rome which seems never to stop, you can finally unwind, if only for a short time. It's almost as if you'd pressed a giant mute button after walking through the door.

The look of Babington's hasn't changed much in more than a century. Graceful palms, dark woods and British prints all contribute to its cozy Victorian aura. When Anna Babington

Courtesy of Babington's

opened her doors to Rome, she had a small black and white cat at her side. Through the years that fabulous feline has been succeeded by a whole dynasty of terrific tabbies, and recently has

continued on page 83

become the official trademark of the tearoom.

When I was first taken to Babington's by a friend, he told me that not only had the tearoom remained open through the rise of Mussolini and World War II, but a small room in the back had been used as a meeting place for members of the Resistance. Babington's may not have always been an island of calm, at least not in those terrible days.

Aside from a selection of more than 100 different teas and the usual itsy, bitsy cucumber sandwiches, if you stop by for breakfast they offer pancakes and fresh scones, with or without tea. Be warned however, Babington's is not for the faint of wallet. The prices are higher than St. Peter's dome.

BABINGTON'S/ PIAZZA DI SPAGNA 23/ TEL: 06-678-6027
Very Expensive

BABINGTON'S MILIEU

The Spanish Steps, all 138 of them, afford countless opportunities to ascend to the Hotel Hassler, or descend into the Piazza di Spagne where thousands of boutiques and cafés beckon. Or how about a drink and some people-watching in the Hassler's elegant lobby lounge? After all that tea, I'm sure you could use a more spirited beverage.

Rome/
Front Burner

IL PAGLIACCIO

Not exactly new but recently updated, those who have taken a fresh look have come away singing Pagliaccio's praises. Chef Anthony Genovese has a menu which fuses together Italian and Asian, no easy task, to create his signature cuisine.

IL PAGLIACCIO/ VIA DEI BANCHI VECCHI 129/
TEL: 06-688-09-595

DITIRAMBO

It may look rustic like a country inn you might find outside of Rome but don't let that fool you. Ditirambo is as of the moment as they come. The specialties are a far cry from your mother's spaghetti and meatballs. If you order pasta, it comes with a rabbit ragu. If you order a simple octopus salad it comes with a purée of white beans and if you order steak it's been sautéed in balsamic vinegar. *Ditirambo* roughly translated means "born from a different experience." They're not kidding.

DITIRAMBO/ PIAZZA DELLA CANCELLERIA 73/
COMPO DE FIORI/ TEL: 06-687-1626

Neptune Fountain in Piazza Nettuno

Bologna/
Detour

"This intended route was far from being the most direct, the one which would have best suited Phileas Fogg"

—Jules Verne

Bologna certainly would not have qualified as the most direct or even remotely direct route to have suited Fogg in his relentless battle with time. But as for me, Bologna is one of the more delicious detours in all of Italy, and not to be missed.

Fans of Jenny Craig or the Nutrisystem method of self-denial should read no further. Bologna is described by its own population as "Bologna la Grassa," meaning "Bologna the Fat." And since my detour has much more to do with self-indulgence than calorie counting, you may want to avoid this city rather than risk a head-on confrontation with an unforgettable platter of tortellini. However, if you can throw caution and your defibrillator to the wind, you're in for a unique experience. Bologna is ground zero for traveling gastronauts.

Prosciutto di Parma

An almost perfectly preserved historical city, Bologna is in the Emilia-Romagna region, considered to be the breadbasket of Italy. The area overflows with gustatory delights inspired by the sheer abundance taken from the land.

The *prosciutto di Parma* smoked in the Emilia-Romagna has a distinctive delicacy, in part due to the lack of pollution in the air that's used to dry it. Romagna's other smoked meats and its exquisite cheeses are exported the world over. However, there's more than enough left over for the countless restaurants of the city to throw together a decent scaloppini or two.

The first thing that I noticed in Bologna were the covered walkways (there are over 40 kilometers of them) called *portici*, lined with stone Corinthian columns. The columns, originally wood, were built during the Renaissance to

continued on page 88

protect the poor from the elements (the rich, you can be sure, had door to door carriage service). And so you might say that most of the city is weatherproof. Pity the unfortunate umbrella manufacturer who was forced to declare bankruptcy in Bologna waiting for customers.

Little did the Bolognese know back in the Renaissance they were creating one of the world's first shopping malls. Many restaurants are tucked under the city's vaulted ceilings, and the

arcades also shelter an assortment of expensive boutiques that are almost as tempting as Bologna's homemade mortadella.

Yet another claim to Bologna's fame is that it is home to Europe's oldest university, established in 1088. The illustrious alumni include Dante, Petrarch, Copernicus and much, much, much later, Fellini. Can you imagine what their senior proms must have been like?

I CARRACCI – #24

Had the Carracci, a family of artists who painted up a storm in the 16th and 17th centuries, but known that their fame would live on into the 21st they would have been immensely cheered. Carracci frescos were commissioned to celebrate the four seasons on the ceilings of the Fava-

Photo by Brandi Sims

Ghisilieri Palace, which later became the seminary of the Archbishop of Bologna, and today is a restaurant bearing the artists' name. The effect is of a mini Sistine Chapel accompanied by a menu. Actually, I've always thought that the addition of a tiny café in the genuine *Cappella Sistina* would

I CARRACCI'S MILIEU

Chances are if you're in Bologna and you're not eating, than you must be exploring the 40 kilometres of arcades filled with shops, food, galleries, theaters and on and on. Best of all, you don't even have to worry about the rain. Or, you can wander the palatial rooms in the rest of the Hotel Baglioni to explore its art collections, including more of those glorious frescos.

have made Michelangelo happy. He almost never got to go out for lunch. Today, it's a toss up as to which is more exciting, the food or the frescos. Still there's no doubt that frescos add a divine touch to the menu.

When I was last in Bologna I stayed at the Hotel Baglioni which shares the palace with I Carracci. Most people who stop at the hotel just assume that I Carracci is the hotel restaurant but in truth it has become a landmark in its own right. The menu is a showcase for Bologna's fabulous local ingredients, and I Carracci has made its sauce Bolognese a three-star event, especially when lavished over a plate of its house-made pasta. Their hand-made pastas are hand-rolled or stuffed, and then transformed by the kitchen into a number of memorable dishes. End your meal with a simple plate of figs picked in the morning and drizzled with aged balsamic vinegar from Modena to underscore the sweetness of the fruit.

I CARRACCI/ VIA MANZONI 2/ TEL: 051-222-049
Moderate

Bologna/
Front Burner

MARCO FADIGA BISTROT

In New York, graffiti covered walls usually denote an abandoned building or subway car but in Bologna graffiti cover the walls at this trendy trattoria. The young chef-owner uses a chalkboard to jot down his latest additions to the *Cucina Moderna* movement. His fans (and they are many) crowd in to sample salmon marinated in coffee and bass tartare with a mango salsa. Chef Boyardee would be shocked!

MARCO FADIGA BISTROT/ VIA RIALTO 23-C/ TEL: 051-220-118

Venice/
Detour

If I was confounded by the fact that Phileas simply would not make time for a quick look at Rome or Bologna, then color me exasperated at his ability to ignore Venice, a fabled city for all time. No one should ever put a foot on Italian soil without giving some serious thought to the pure joy that comes from floating down one of Venice's idyllic canals. At least before—as most of its residents fear—it's swallowed up by the waves of the Adriatic. Even the most optimistic environmentalists think Venice's future is a watery one. Today, when you get a sinking feeling in Venice it's not an emotional response; it's a grim reality. This exquisite city is sinking inch by inch every year. When I last visited Venice I was alarmed to see the water lapping hungrily at the terrace of the Hotel Gritti Palace—an elitist recollection to be sure but also a frightening one. Try as they might, a legion of engineers from all over the world failed to come up with a lasting solution, so it may be going, going glub-glub for this astonishing city.

Most travelers have two very distinct responses to Venice. One is disbelief at the beauty of this almost mythic setting. The other is disbelief at the fragrance of the city's canals and the assorted garbage left to rot in the sun of Piazza San Marco. Some visitors are also repelled by the crush of the seasonal crowds and the hordes of pigeons, alarmingly focused on your edibles. The naysayers see Venice as if it were a board game, and the visitor who can amass the most unhygienic, unpleasant experiences, wins. It amazes me that anyone would spend time sniffing the canals when she or he could be enjoying the way that the water mirrors back the sheer magnificence of Venice. What a sin!

It would be easy to think of Venice as a huge stage set that's rolled out during the summer months for the benefit of the thundering herd and then taken apart in the fall to be stored until next year. But the truth is that behind all that gilded scenery, Venice has a thriving backstage community who calls this waterlogged city home. Many of the families who live and work in Venice have been there for centuries. Today the city's pressing problem, aside from rising water levels and yearly tourist invasion, is that more and more young Venetians have chosen to move to drier land. Or perhaps it's just that they no longer want to remain in what has become a Renaissance theme park for visitors. Even some diehards fear that soon there will be no way to keep the sea out and the city afloat. *Death in Venice* resonates not as the title of a literary classic but as a macabre prediction.

It seems particularly ironic that Venice, a powerful city-state during the Renaissance and the world's showcase for Byzantine opulence, should now be at the mercy of its own touristic success. If the doges (rulers) had realized when they created one of the most civilized and feared empires that it would be remembered by tour guides as the birthplace of the venetian blind or the city that introduced sugar to the rest of Europe, they might not have bothered.

Though there are glorious churches, fascinating museums and historic palaces to visit, it almost seems an intrusion to do anything in Venice aside from spending hour after hour at one of its many cafes. If the café is in Piazza San Marco, then the usual activity is sipping a Cinzano and nibbling on a *crostini* while listening to one of many outdoor orchestras play *Fascination*. The crumbs left from the *crostini* are fair game for the only creatures actually entitled to be called pigeon-toed, those cheeky birds who make the square their parade ground. As your glass empties, you order yet another Cinzano to sip as the sun goes down. I can't think of a more sybaritic way to "see" Venice.

It may have the Grand Canal but Venice doesn't always match it up with Grand Cuisine. Venice is much more about sight than taste.

Of all the Italian cities noted for their brilliant *cucinas*, Venice usually finds itself somewhere in the middle—not the most revered, but not the most disregarded, either. With a bit of detective work you can find a restaurant gem or two tucked into one of the city's narrow alleys. When I'm forced to take nourishment, I regretfully leave Piazza San Marco with its haunting strains of *Fascination*, and head for an aromatic bowl of *zuppa di pesce*, which is just another way to order a fine kettle of fish at al Graspo de Ua.

GRASPO DE UA – #25

Always teeming with people who seem to linger for hours, methodically shelling their mussels and clams, Graspo de Ua is a Venetian fish story. But unlike most fish stories, this one is no exaggeration. The display that greeted me when I entered would have made Neptune take a second look. Part of the attraction, aside from the marine visuals, is that Graspo de Ua (bunch of grapes) has made its reputation with the locals, not just the invaders. There are restaurants on every street in Venice filled with non-Venetians, and so a more hometown atmosphere seems to make everything taste better. And Graspo's sunny yellow walls under the dark beamed ceilings make for a warm, comfy setting. To top it all off there are Italian proverbs stenciled on the beams that run the gamut in translation from, "Bread and wine bring happiness" to "Wine is the best medicine." No argument from me in either case. Most of the Italian words are understandable—even so my waiter took a special delight in translating them for me. That almost never happens at Applebee's.

Whatever the catch of the day is, it turns up on the menu at Graspo for lunch or dinner. You can smell the perfume of the Adriatic still clinging to its most precious possessions, as if unwilling to give up even a single scallop. The menu, while starring the denizens of the deep, also has a variety of risottos, some with seafood, some with wild mushrooms, all rich as Croesus. If you find it compelling, as I do, to actually order *fegato alla Veneziana* right in *Venezia*, this is your big chance. Liver and onions, as it's referred to in the States, was a staple of luncheonette menus. But at Graspo, it's not just liver and onions, it's *delicioso* and worth ordering even if the restaurant specializes in seafood. After all, who's to know that you didn't explore the cuttlefish in its own ink, or the flounder stuffed with octopus? Trust me—I'm not just whistling "Tosca" here.

GRASPO DE UA /CALLE DEI BOMBASERI/ TEL: 39-520-0150
Moderate

GRASPO DE UA'S MILIEU

What to do next? It's as obvious as a gondola on 42ⁿᵈ Street. Since Calle dei Bombaseri, the narrow street that Graspo de Ua calls home, opens on to the Rialto, it's only a short distance to Ca' d'Oro. That would be the magnificent palazzo where Venice's doges hung their jeweled hats. When Ca' d'Oro was built in the 15ᵗʰ century, its façade was completely gilded so that it could reflect the sun. Architectural Digest, eat your heart out. The Moorish influences make the courtyard seem like a side trip to Istanbul. You'll also find the Galleria Franchetti which has some exquisite examples of Renaissance art.

If Ca' d'Oro is closed, then try an evening stroll under the Rialto Bridge. It will give you an opportunity to pick up all those tacky souvenirs you wouldn't be caught dead buying in the light of day.

HARRY'S BAR – #26

So, who is this famous Harry and why does he have all those bars? No matter where you go these days there's a Harry's Bar, even Tokyo, and no matter how hard you try, you can't see the Grand Canal. The answer to the often asked question has, in fact, no answer. If you think about it, there would have to be countless Harry's to run all of those bars. And so, while the stories and explanations are as numerous as its drink choices, Harry's remains an enigma wrapped in an enigma. All the other Harry's may have some sort of family connection. but the legendary watering hole in

Venice is in a class by itself.

To get back to the first Harry---historically speaking, the original cast of characters did include a Cipriani. It was Arrigo Cipriani, Harry's dad, who first had the impossible dream. The story goes that in the '20s Arrigo was a bartender in one of the elegant hotels on the Grand Canal that catered to the beautiful people who made Venice their personal playground. Enter a man named Harry (there's that name again) Pickering, a fabulously rich American who made a habit of having Arrigo whip up his drink *del giorno*. After a while, Harry Pickering became a friend as well as a fixture. It came as a shock to Arrigo when one day Harry disappeared. He then reappeared weeks later, and admitted that he had gone through all his lira. The hotel staff had begun to chase him down hallways, waving his, by now, gigantic bill. Without even a break in the rhythm of his cocktail shaker, Arrigo scraped together enough money to rescue his friend. Though this is beginning to verge on the operatic, hang in there, it really will be worth it.

Pages fall from the calendar and a year or two later who should walk into Arrigo's bar? You guessed it. Harry had returned. He not only paid his debt, but he added a handsome bonus in gratitude. He said that he had always wanted his very own bar (Are you getting the connection?) and asked Arrigo to be his partner. Drum roll!

Harry's Bar opened in 1931. and from that moment on Harry Pickering sat in a chair in the corner and greeted everyone who came through the door. In no time Harry's became the place to be in Venice, and Arrigo ruled his territory behind the bar with the elegance of a doge. The bottom line is: Who really knows what makes a room with a few tables, chairs and a convivial atmosphere become a legend? Whatever that illusive quality may have been, Harry's Bar became a magnet for a host of boldface names. Hemmingway and Bogart had martini contests (my bet is it ended in a draw), Noel and Gertie turned up for their five o'clock Bellinis, and the Aga Khan found Harry's tiny grilled cheese sandwiches almost as satisfying as a new prayer rug. Those very sandwiches are still on the menu and, as far as I'm concerned, still as addictive.

Today, the world has moved on and so have the crowned heads and celebs who used to appear at Harry's with regularity, even Brad and Angelina.

Like most of the landmarks in Venice, Harry's has succumbed to the crush of humanity. Recently the management was driven to impose a *no shorts* dress code, where once a white dinner jacket was considered informal. I must admit that before I stop in at Harry's I can't help but rummage through my suitcase for something that twinkles or floats, just for old time sake. It's the Joan Crawford in me rising to the surface, and Harry's is still the perfect place to flaunt her.

Now that Harry's days as a pit stop for the rich and richer have passed, you would think that booking a table or at least finding a spot at the bar would be a cinch. Forgedddabouditt! Harry's is still jammed every night, only now it's with thirsty backpackers. The poor misguided souls who try to crowd through the door won't be rewarded with anything but aching tootsies. The wait can take you from one season to the next. A reservation is crucial unless you want to lean against the bar or lean against the people already leaning against the bar. A word to all the frugalistas, if you don't have your Bellini or Compari while seated, you won't get charged for service or tax. Don't try a seven course meal this way but today every little Euro helps.

If you do decide to reserve a table for lunch or dinner you will eat very well. Amidst all of the hub and the bub, Harry's turns out a terrific plate of pasta. The fish is moist and perfectly done, the *carpaccio* (razor thin sliced prime beef served with a caper sauce) is a house specialty and it should be. It's marvelous. The biggest relief of all is that the service is still deft and stylish. All of this may or may not be worth its weight in gold, which is what you'll wind up paying. That said, there is simply no way to visit Venice without stopping in at Harry's Bar for a drink, a toasted cheese sandwich and a large helping of its mystique.

HARRY'S BAR/ CALLE VALLARESSO, 1323/ TEL: 41-528-5777
Super Expensive

THE HOTEL CIPRIANI /THE BAR – #27

Why not leave the Piazza San Marco, and head to the Piazzetta (the small square) and onto the Grand Canal. Proceed along the Canal waterfront to the motor boats tied up at dockside, almost opposite the Doge's Palace. Think adventure. You're on your way to one of the most glamorous nightcaps in Venice.

A few steps away from the Doge's Palace, give or take, you will see a small canopy marked Hotel Cipriani at the dock. Your adventure is about to begin. A devastatingly handsome Venetian, dressed in a snazzy yachting outfit, will ask if you want to be taken out to the hotel. This does not involve a change of accommodation, merely a fieldtrip to explore the fabled Hotel Cipriani and perhaps stop for a drink. Cipriani is located on one of the small islands (Giudecca) right across the Grand Canal—you get to use the hotel motor launch as your transportation. It's just a four minute voyage but oh, what a magical ride it is.

As you pull away from the dock, you have all of Venice in your sight. The closer you get to the hotel the more ravishing the view behind you becomes. Actually, you're seeing Venice the same way that ships arriving at the time of the Renaissance did. Can you imagine how impressive Venice at the height if its power must have been? And of course, how impressive it will be when you return after your drink. There are people who stay at the Cipriani, not just because it's considered to be one of the world's great hotels, but because of the boat ride. I must confess that I'm one of them. Being ferried back and forth in such luxury is a great persuader.

The Cipriani was just a small inn when Arrigo Cipriani decided in the late '30s to expand his holdings and buy it. The inn's location was perfect since it was tucked away overlooking a quiet lagoon and all the rooms had views of the water. Over the years as the inn became better known it also became less tucked. Its reputation for luxury and service rivaled the Gritti Palace, Venice's première Grand Dame, and was soon discovered by Europe's elite. The simple little inn has grown through the years to have 100 rooms, an Olympic-size swimming pool and a tennis court (one would think a dangerous sport in Venice).

There are two bars at the "Cip" (pronounced *chip* in Italian). The Fortuny bar is my favorite. It's lush with velvets, paintings and dark wood, and it overlooks the gardens and the lagoon beyond. It's the perfect place for lingering over a Bellini (yes, they serve them there, too).

The Fortuny restaurant is smashing in décor, done with a domed ceiling not unlike a mini St. Peter's (I'm not sure if the pope has been told yet), and is aglitter with Venetian glass. The terrace rolls out into the flower-filled gardens and it, too, overlooks the lagoon. All in all, the setting is 24-carat. The food, while quite good, requires a Swiss bank account or alternatively a mask and a gun to pay the bill. Since billionaires routinely stop at the Cip just breathing the same air can make your portfolio much more bullish. Although it's done up in the grand manner, the Fortuny restaurant is really no substitute for the fun of dining back in the "real" Venice.

HOTEL CIPRIANI/ ISOLA GIUDECCA/ TEL: 41-
520-7744
Very Very Expensive

CAFFÉ FLORIAN – #28

Now that you're back on semi-dry land again, it seems much too early to say goodnight to Venice, especially with all those orchestras still playing to a hypnotized crowd. How about a cup of chocolate or a cappuccino and a small *cannoli* along with the music?

Caffé Florian opened its doors in 1720. The

owners have taken great pains to preserve its history, and that would be history with a capital H. Florian is believed to be one of the oldest coffee houses in the world.

With its stained glass windows,

gilded walls, plush upholstery and frescoed ceilings, Florian exudes the Venetian elegance of the past. For nearly 300 years almost everyone who has passed through Venice has stopped for a large helping of the latest gossip and intrigue along with refreshment. Florian was Casanova's favorite spot to preview the beauties of the day. He must have had a really outstanding time since it was the only *caffé* in Venice that served women.

One of the several rooms at Florian is named "The Room of Illustrious Men," and that's no joke. The room is filled with heroic paintings of Marco Polo, Titian, Palladio and Goldoni, although some of them were not around in time to have been Florian regulars. The luckier ones who turned up for a dish of *sorbetto* include Oscar Wilde, Dickens, Eleanora Dusa, Modigliani and Proust, who had to settle for a *biscotto* instead of a *madeleine*.

Photo by karlakp

CAFFÉ FLORIAN / PIAZZA SAN MARCO 56/ TEL:
   41-520-5641
Moderate

CAFFÉ FLORIAN'S MILIEU

If by now you're sick of hearing Fascination *and downing Cinzano in Piazza San Marco, rise from your chair and walk across the square to the Campanile (bell tower). The first thing to understand about the Campanile is that it's a phony. I know, that sounds rather harsh, especially since most of Venice is in pretty good shape, at least the areas still above the waterline.*

The Venetians call their tower "the master of the house" since it towers over everything in a protective manner. Their perception is somewhat ironic. The Campanile, built in 1513, suffered from somewhat less than first rate construction, and in 1904 just crumbled to the ground in a mountain of rubble. Not to be daunted, the Venetians rebuilt it, and it continues to stand as one of the most famous symbols of the Venetian empire. When I was last there, you could climb to the top of the tower for a spectacular view. But today, security considerations have made the Campanile off limits.

Venice/
Front Burner

LE BISTROT DE VENISE

Le Bistrot is a combination art gallery, poetry center, wine tasting room and café. It's the perfect place to write postcards and have an espresso. But that's not all. If you come for dinner you may be treated to some of its 15th century Venetian classic recipes, taken from its 15th century Venetian cookbooks. How cool is that?

LE BISTROT DE VENISE/ SAN MARCO 4685/
TEL: 41-523-6651

Bombay/Mumbai/
Detour

"In which Phileas Fogg travels the whole length of the Ganges without thinking it worth a look."

—Jules Verne

PHILEAS MIGHT HAVE THOUGHT AS The Mongolia steamed toward Bombay, that the sacred River Ganges wasn't worth even a glance. I, on the other hand, while not quite ready to bathe in it or have my ashes strewn upon it, did, in fact, notice it when I visited India. As for Phileas, cleansing himself in the waters of the Ganges was simply not on his itinerary. Absolution from his sins didn't really apply to our intrepid traveler. He was never in one place long enough to commit any major transgressions, except for one, and in my opinion, a lulu; he never stopped long enough to enjoy any of the extraordinary places he visited in the course of his journey.

Not so for Mark Twain, who was an avid traveler. After touring India in the 1890s he said, "So far as I am able to judge, nothing has been left undone, either by man or nature, to make India the most extraordinary country that the sun visits on his rounds."

True to form, Phileas, once deposited on the shores of Bombay, made a beeline

Left: The Ganges River passes through Varnasi (formerly known as Benares).

to the train station to book passage for Calcutta, leaving himself with only a measly four hours to spare before his next departure. Passepartout took the time to sightsee, so to speak, but bungled his visit to a temple by belligerently refusing to part with his shoes. By the time Fogg bailed his servant out of jail, there was not time even for a hurried curry before boarding their train. What follows is some of what Fogg missed.

If Phileas had arrived in Bombay, not in the 1800s but in the last few years, even *he* would have noticed that "Bombay," as Europeans had once understood the name of the key Arabian Sea port city to be, had changed to "Mumbai." I first visited India after the name change or reversion took place, but it was obvious that not all the population delighted to embrace "Mumbai." Many slipped back to Bombay, as the city had been known to much of the world for the last few hundred years.

Bombay's segue into Mumbai was officially in praise of the goddess Mumbaidevi. Little by little over the last half century, there has been a real effort to replace most European designations of public buildings with Hindu names. However, no one seems particularly worried about enforcing India's nationalistic naming, and so half the population just uses whatever is most familiar.

Mumbai's British connection started back in 1661, when Charles II and his bride, Catherine of Portugal, were given the seven small islands of Bombay as a wedding present. Even though Charles was, at the time, unimpressed, everyone agreed that it was better than getting yet another toaster. Had the islands been kept by Catherine's father, instead of wrapped as a gift, everyone in Mumbai might be speaking Portuguese and eating feijoada.

Bombay or Mumbai is India's most populous city and to me sometimes seems overwhelming. Think noise, color, traffic, chaos, bazaars, temples, flowers, garbage, animals, beggars, hawkers, pollution, luxury, poverty, palaces, markets and the sheer enormity of its ever growing population. With over 14 million Mumbaikars (yes, that's what they're called), almost anything might happen.

Mumbai seems the emotional center of India, no matter how Calcutta and Delhi prosper and grow. That became more apparent after the shock of the 2008 attack by terrorists. The devastating siege by the terrorists lasted three days and by the time it was over 173 people were dead and 308 wounded. Much of the destruction took place at one of Mumbai's landmark hotels, The Taj Mahal Palace. Other attacked sites include the Oberoi Hotel near the Taj and the Victoria Rail Station, another landmark.

I watched the TV coverage in disbelief while smoke billowed from the blackened windows of the Taj. As it was with New York after 9/11, there was an enormous outpouring of sympathy and support, not only from the rest of India but from all over the world. When two years later, I asked the staff at the Taj how they returned to normal after such a shattering trauma, they told me that through the years bombings have become a way of life in India, and life must go on. The only overt reminder of the disaster at the hotel is a small, glassed-in waterfall and a stone plaque bearing the names of those who were lost.

On a much less somber note, Mumbai is not only the home of the Indian Stock Exchange, but also the home of Bollywood, India's remarkable film industry and a source of immense national pride. Today the city is all about money and movies, two things that have always been an unbeatable combination. Both have added boatloads of rupees to the Indian economy.

Bollywood, with its antic film community, has picked up the gauntlet dropped by the dream merchants of Hollywood and raised it to dizzying new heights. Famous for epic productions that are a combination of Arabian Nights fantasies and Busby Berkeley musicals, Bollywood has elevated Mumbai to the pinnacle of Asian glamour. You can book a tour to most of the Bollywood studios. Just ask at your hotel.

Many first time American travelers to India have sampled Indian cuisine at their local all-you-can-eat buffets. The one-size-fits-all menus most resemble the old chop suey joints that were the rage when only Marco Polo could afford a trip to China.

Bollywood musical scene

In reality, Indian cuisine is as varied and complicated as India itself. The British thought that Indian food was anything that was made with curry leaves from the curry tree along with other spices. They were only partially right. The curry leaves are used in regional Indian cooking. But, in fact, the word curry roughly translated means "gravy," and can be made with any combination of spices and herbs such as coriander, fenugreek,

Samosas are a tasty street food.

turmeric, cumin and red pepper. Curries can be incendiary, merely blistering or mild and sweet, and they're used in the preparation of meat, fish, vegetables or chicken. The versatility of curries is seemingly endless.

The Indian palate is expanding by leaps and bounds. In Mumbai, as in New York, the restaurant buzz is to be savored like fine wine. But that's not to say that religious food taboos are completely off the menu. Many devout Hindus still abstain from beef, and Mumbaikars transplanted from the south of India prefer a vegetarian diet. As for the Muslim population, pork for many is still forbidden fruit, and other dietary restrictions continue to be honored.

There is no one culinary tradition that is identified with Mumbai. Countless cuisines that represent every city, region, culture and climate in India can be found here. What has changed of late is the rise of the five-star luxury restaurant to match the excellence of Mumbai's five-star luxury hotels. Instead of the boring continental dining rooms that were once found in their lobbies, hotels have begun to trust the fact that their native cuisine is increasingly popular with their foreign guests.

On the other hand, if you're a firm believer in adventure as the spice of life, then all you have to do is follow your nose. The perfume of the streets in Mumbai is the aroma of deep fried *samosas*—tiny pastry triangles filled with meat or veggies—or tiny kebabs that you can nibble as you stroll. The people of Mumbai seem to suffer from the munchies whenever they leave home. There are also food stalls that overflow with freshly roasted peanuts and lentils to be scooped up with *chapatti*, a wheat bread cooked on a small griddle. All of this street food comes under the category of *chaats* or snacks. But that's only the beginning. Then there are super sweet Indian confections, the fresh fruit juices and *lassi*, the velvety yoghurt drink, to put out the fire from anything containing those dynamite chilies. Wherever you, look people are snacking and talking and laughing. Mumbai is a vast banquet of delectable choices and Mumbaikars are eager to try them all.

MASALA KRAFT – #29

Tucked into the first floor of the sumptuous Taj Mahal Palace, one would never expect the clean lines and simple setting of Masala Kraft. But appearances can be deceptive. Judging from the variety of contemporary Indian dishes that come from its kitchen, Masala Kraft is Mumbai Central for "nouvelle Indian" cuisine, as designed by Executive Chef Hemant Oberoi, the mastermind behind most of the Taj Group's restaurants.

Masala is a blend of spices, usually curry leaves, cardamom, cloves, pepper etc, and can be mega-hot or more moderately spiced. Garam masala is the mixture that's most familiar to the western palate. At Masala Kraft, Chef Oberoi has used his own masala blends to put an innovative spin on Indian cuisine. Oberoi joined the Taj group in 1986 and today oversees 10 of its prestigious restaurants. His dedication to the lighter side of Indian gastronomy translates into cooking

Courtesy of Masala Kraft

with pure olive oil instead of the traditional ghee (clarified butter), an absence of heavy cream and thick sauces. Chef Oberoi uses only the freshest spices and herbs. The result is a combination of subtle flavors and subdued heat.

Dinner at Masala Kraft starts with a quick dip of the hands into fragrant rose water. After that the bread trolley adds the aroma of freshly baked *phulkas* (puffed Indian breads cooked over an open flame) to the table. Then on to delicate lentil dumplings drizzled with a ginger and date relish. Lamb kebabs, unbelievably delicate and moist, were, I was told, originally made for India's former Mughal rulers who loved eating but disliked aggressive chewing. (Obviously, Wrigley's would have gone bankrupt had it depended on the upper classes of India.) Next I was brought a slab of pink salmon, baked to a succulent turn in the tandoor oven and glazed with a tangy sugarcane vinegar. The salmon was paired with one of Masala Kraft's brilliant vegetarian choices, *Aloo ki Katlian*, a sliced potato, perfumed with cumin, and spiced with chilies and curry leaves. Indian food means never having to wear your Chanel No. 5; no one would be able to appreciate it. And for dessert, *kulfi*, a dense, triple-rich frozen cream.

MASALA KRAFT/ TAJ MAHAL PALACE/ APOLLO
    BUNDER/ COLABA/ TEL: 22-5665-3366
Moderate

Taj Mahal Palace, left; *Gateway of India,* right

MASALA KRAFT'S MILIEU

There are so many choices for exploration in the area, pre or post Masala Kraft, but none is more captivating than a walk around the Taj hotel itself. Despite its name, the Taj was never a palace except in the luxurious sense of the word. Dating back to 1903, it's a lush combination of Moorish, Oriental and Florentine architecture. Somehow they all work together to produce a monumental structure that is both imposing and fanciful. The Taj is divided into the original building and a much more modern tower addition. The "palace" rooms are filled with antiques and irreplaceable art works.

Have a Turkish coffee and a slice of baklava at the Souk Restaurant Colaba, the Taj Mahal's atmospheric rooftop restaurant. It has a smashing view of the Gateway of India.

Construction of the Gateway of India began in 1911 to celebrate a visit by King George V and Queen Mary. Since it wasn't finished until 1924, the British royal couple had to be content with a cardboard model. So much for planning ahead. Today the Gateway is a favorite gathering place for both locals and visitors who come for the magnificent view and perhaps a sandwich or an ice cream cone. Most of the time, scores of milling vendors outnumber their customers. At night the Gateway is illuminated, which only adds to its glorious presence.

INDIGO – #30

As I stepped through the door into Indigo and looked around, it seemed to be crowded with all the beautiful people of Mumbai. Elegant saris were accessorized with Hermes bags, Jimmy Choo shoes and strikingly handsome men. My heart (and possibly my reputation) was sinking. Had I mistakenly come to some continental hotspot when my mission was to explore the best of Indian cuisine?

Was I breaking my own rule about not going to European restaurants when in non European countries? Well, maybe just a teensy tiny bit. After all, what good are rules if you don't break them when strongly advised to do so? I had heard about Indigo from those in the know in Mumbai's restaurant world, and I felt it was my duty as an equal opportunity diner to see and taste for myself.

Indigo, as I soon found out in the most scrumptious of ways, is a legitimately important and acclaimed restaurant in Mumbai, and not just another pretty menu.

Indigo's chef, Rahul Akerkar, is a superstar throughout India and beyond. In his kitchen, amid the pots and pans, hang the many awards he's been given over the years by international food critics and publications, among them *Condé*

INDIGO'S MILIEU

Now that you've had a chance to soak up the haute glam of Indigo, it might be just the time to look for a shopping bargain to make up for losing all those rupees at the restaurant. Happily, you're in the right area. Colaba is known for its endless budget shopping choices in ethnic arts and crafts. The main street for browsing is the Mohammed Ali Road.

Nast Traveler, who named Indigo as one of the 60 finest restaurants in the world.

It seems that Indigo's fame has spread from Bollywood to Hollywood and back. Celebs from everywhere have turned up to sample Akerkar's luscious, fusion creations. The waiter may whisper softly about Katie and Tom, Hill and Bill or the cast of *Slumdog Millionaire*, while taking your order. Mine started with Roasted Mushroom and Coconut Soup scented with lemongrass and almonds. One of the most asked-for dishes on the menu is the Lobster Risotto with Black Olive Tapanade. The lobster made for an extra rich risotto and added a whiff of the sea. Roasted Spiced Beets lounged next to caramelized pears dusted with shallots. For dessert, a chocolate fondant (triple thick mousse) flavored with jalapeños, just for a kick.

If at all possible, try to be seated in Indigo's outdoor terrace up on the second floor. The frangipani trees, laden with blossoms, droop down over the tables and make for a truly romantic atmosphere. Akerkar, unlike most chefs who try to enhance their menus with new and seasonal specialties, changes his menu about once a year, showing a confidence that comes from knowing you're the best.

INDIGO/ 4 MANDLIK HOUSE/ APOLLO BANDAR/ TEL: 22-6636-8999
Expensive

TRISHNA – #31

If I had to compare the incomparable Trishna to anything, anywhere, it would have to be Le Bernardin in New York. Both are iconic restaurants, dedicated to serving fabulous fish. Bernardin is an impressive tummy temple housed in elegant surroundings and often filled with CEOs from every major corporation in Manhattan. Trishna is a rundown, slightly seedy joint with waiters who are indifferent enough to work at any Jewish deli. Ambiance aside, Trishna is a place for people who think of fish as more than just a way to ingest their Omega 3s. It caters to serious "affishanados."

No matter when you arrive, Trishna is always stuffed to the gills with the greats and the near greats of Mumbai. And wherever you look, there are plates overflowing with giant king crabs (the specialty) being dissected with the utmost finesse.

TRISHNA'S MILIEU

Trishna is in an area called Kala Ghoda. One of the more interesting of the many impressive buildings found in Kala Ghoda is the Prince of Wales Museum, now named Chhatrapati Shivaji Maharaj Vastu Sangrahalaya. The museum is known for its collection of miniature paintings. Nearby is the Rajabai Clock Tower with its imposing Gothic-style as well as the very Victorian Army and Navy building.

If wrestling with a giant sea monster is not your cup of chai then Trishna has succulent tiger prawns done in whatever manner you decide and heaped on the plate in mountainous piles. The pomfret, a small delicate fish found in the Indian Ocean, is baked in the tandoor oven and served with a fragrant green masala.

Desserts at Trishna should be regarded as just an afterthought, so don't bother to leave room for them, just have another plate of prawns instead.

TRISHNA/ BIRLA MANSION, SAI BABA MARG, KALA GHODA, FORT ROAD/ TEL: 22-2270-3214
Moderate

Mumbai/
Front Burner

KHYBER

Khyber is *the* place to go in Mumbai for Mughlai cuisine, the food of the old rulers of northern India. The atmosphere is exotic and the traditional flavors of anise, ginger and yoghurt, lend a delicacy to the food. The restaurant, spread out over three floors of white marble, frescos and wooden beams, has servers in traditional costume.

Khyber's menu includes a variety of kebabs and bhutta Masala, a northern curry specialty, served with fragrant rotis fresh from Khyber's ovens.

KHYBER/ 145 M.G.ROAD, FORT/ TEL: 22-2267-3227

THE OLIVE BAR AND KITCHEN

Bollywood meets Foie Gras and the result is that Olive's is the coooolest place to be, especially on Thursday nights. That's when Olive's dance music reverberates off its whitewashed walls. To add to its coolness, Manu Chandra, who returned to Mumbai after appearing in some of New York's top kitchens, turns out Mediterranean delicacies accompanied by a very *au courant* martini menu.

OLIVE BAR AND KITCHEN/ PALI HILL TOURIST HOTEL 14/ UNION PARK, 14 KHAR/ TEL: 22-2605-8228

Delhi/
Detour

Delhi is a tale of not two but many cities. Two wouldn't begin to explain the different periods and cultures that went into making Delhi what it is today. As with the street scene in Mumbai, Delhi is choked with wall-to-wall humanity. Its population is now counted at roughly 13,000,000. Go with the flow, it may actually save your sanity, not to mention your well-being in Delhi's most crowded areas. In any case, you may not have any other choice.

The Hindus, then the Muslims added their signatures to the rich and diverse history of Delhi. It was in 1649 that Delhi became the Mughal capital of India. It wasn't until the 18th and 19th centuries that the head honchos of the British East India Company decided they liked curry even more than fish and chips, and gained complete control of India from its Mughal rulers. In 1858, the English established the Raj with Calcutta as its chief administrative city. But in 1911 George V became convinced that Delhi, not Calcutta, was the place to set up his capital city. It would be the key jewel in his British crown.

And what better way to bring European progress to an ancient and highly developed civilization than to add the word "new" to the capital's name? And so Delhi, with great ceremony but not much citizen enthusiasm became New Delhi. Even though this may seem a somewhat over simplified history of Anglo-Indian relations, the results were entirely predictable. The British as well as the "new" were never really embraced,

Red Fort

and as soon as India achieved its independence in 1947 it was, once again, *Hello,* Delhi.

The city of Delhi seems to have a variety of faces. There's Old Delhi, made up of the seven ancient cities within a city, crowded with bazaars, tiny streets and countless temples and fewer mosques. There's Central Delhi, where the

influence of the British is, even today, strongly felt in its shops and businesses, and then there's New Delhi. It wasn't until the '20s and '30s that most of New Delhi's large neo-classical colonial buildings and sweeping boulevards were laid out in all their post-Victorian grandeur. This part of the city is considered the more cosmopolitan section of Delhi.

The Red Fort, the most dramatic relic left of Delhi's Mughal Empire, is found in the oldest part of the city. It took over ten years to build and was finished in 1648. It was meant to be a vivid symbol of the enormous power of the Mughals but ironically the Fort had even more staying power and outlasted them.

The Red Fort is not a bright, jarring red, it's more of a burnt orange sandstone and looks its most magnificent at sunset when the color deepens. The entrance to the inner court is wide enough for a procession of brilliantly painted pachyderms carrying an endless parade of bejeweled rajahs to the great hall within. In the old days, and I do mean old, the ceiling of the Hall of Private Audience, where the Mughal emperor held court, was made of solid silver. At the time it was valued at more than 12 million pounds sterling. Alas, the silver was stripped off years ago and replaced by white marble. Still, the effect today is hardly chopped liver.

Perhaps the most poignant monument in Old Delhi is the most understated. Raj Ghat, to the south of the Red Fort on the shore of the Yamuna River, is where Gandhi, who was assassinated in 1948, was cremated. His funeral pyre is commemorated by a simple black marble slab.

Central Delhi surely reflects the British more than the city's Indian population. Connaught Place, which dominates the area, is like Étoile in Paris. All of the streets of Central Delhi radiate out from its center to buildings shaded by graceful colonnades. Since the heat can sometimes exceed 100 degrees Fahrenheit, the shade is a welcome relief to the shoppers who crowd the sector's stores and restaurants. As I walked through Connaught Place and looked at the usual mall suspects, it was clear that the place to be was Old Delhi, with its riotous combinations of colors, it's fascinating markets and most of all it's overwhelming humanity, determined to not only survive but to enjoy life no matter how hard the struggle.

Food in Delhi, as in Mumbai, is often food eaten on the streets. The *chaats* or snacks are perfect for anytime of the day. They're also a budgetary blessing for people who have to watch their rupees. Just a few coins will buy a juicy kebab or a fragrant *samosa*. For the traveler who decides to try some of Delhi's irresistible street food, its wise to pick your vendor with an eye to what can be cooked right in front of you. Usually the ingredients are fresh and cooking helps to ward off local bacteria that might be off limits to a traveling tummy. Another tip from a friend who visits India regularly is to carry a few small paper plates with you. Often the problem with street food is not with the food itself, but the water that the vendor's plates have been washed in.

The cuisine that's served in Delhi's restaurants, as in the rest of Northern India, is informed by the influences of the former Mughal empire. The Mughals used the tandoor oven for their meat and fish, and any number of different breads such as *rotis* and *chipatis* (flat), *parathas* (buttered to make a tender, flaky dough) and *phulkas* (stuffed with onions and potatoes). The spices flavoring meat or fish are usually ginger and garlic. That mysterious red color usually associated with tandoori roasting can be as simple as a bit of food coloring. Tandoori selections are traditionally served with pickled vegetables and mint chutney.

In general, Delhi's curries tend to be sweet and mild, nowhere near as fiery as many

Photo by Erin

Chaats on a paper plate in New Delhi

found in Mumbai. The curries are most often made with chicken or lamb though endless vegetarian choices are also popular. Meats are traditionally marinated in yoghurt and spices to make them tender before cooking. The dals or cooked lentils, served as a side dish, also use yoghurt to insure a silky texture.

The all-purpose flatbread, the *chapatti*, is served with most Delhi dishes. It comes straight off the grill, and is brought to the table crisp and piping hot. Another great favorite from the Delhi kitchen is *rogan josh* which is a complex dish made of lamb simmered in yoghurt and a formidable array of spices: cardamom, cayenne, cinnamon, cloves, garlic, bay leaves, coriander, black peppercorns and on and on and on.

Desserts in the north of India are often made with milk, cooked down to a dense cream and then spiced with ginger, mint or pistachios. For the finishing touch, a dessert may be draped with a thin sheet of edible silver. It's the Indian version at a meal's end of a silver lining.

VARQ – #32

During the evening hours, when its lights have been dimmed, Varq seems to glow with an inner candescence. The opulence of the rich woods, a ceiling covered in gold leaf and red lamps over the tables, all serve to heighten Varq's sense of drama.

At Varq, gold has been used not only to make the ceiling shimmer, but chef Amit Chowdhury uses gold to sparkle his elegant food presentations.

Varq is the Indian name for the edible gold and silver leaf used to ornament food.

Chowdhury spent years in London, where he potted around with some of the best chefs in the world. Chowdhury has taken elements from other cultures and translated them to create his unique Indian cuisine.

One of the standouts on the menu is Varqi Crab, crabmeat served wrapped in a parchment thin Greek-style phyllo dough and topped off with a giant tandoori prawn. Delhi meets Athens and the result is spectacular! Another sign that this is no traditional Indian restaurant is the use of palate refreshers, fruit sorbets perfumed with tamarind served between courses.

The chef pairs dishes with specially selected teas served cold or hot. I chose a chilled brew made from rose petals, cinnamon and cloves. Throughout the meal a cart appeared with special breads, among them a very 21st century olive *naan* (flat yeast bread) and a mozzarella *kulcha* (flatbread with potato or onion in the dough). As interpreted by Varq, modern Indian cuisine seems an exciting expansion of India's ancient culinary arts.

Courtesy of Varq

VARQ/ TAJ MAHAL HOTEL/ 1 MANSINGH ROAD/
   TEL: 11-2302-6162
Expensive

VARQ'S MILIEU

Varq is in the Taj Mahal Hotel, on Mansingh Road in an upscale residential area. There really isn't much nearby to walk to after dinner. Of course, the magnificent lobby of the Taj itself is a great place for a drink or a coffee. Another idea might be a cab to Connaught Place which will put you in the middle of Raj territory. The British built the complex in 1931 to have a calm, less crowded place for shopping and strolling, far away from Delhi's crowds. It's still pleasant walking under its cool colonnades, where you can browse, shop or stop for a cup of tea.

Varqi Crab

This luxuriously-flavored recipe has several stages of preparation. The ingredients for each stage, as listed here, can be doubled to make four appetizers.

Phyllo Squares

- *1 sheet phyllo pastry*
- *2 ounces (½ stick) unsalted butter, clarified (see NOTE) or ghee*
- *½ teaspoon ground turmeric*
- *½ teaspoon carom seeds (optional)*

Tandoori Shellfish Marinade

- *2 prawns or large shrimp or crayfish, shell removed and deveined, tail on*
- *½ cup whole milk plain yoghurt*
- *½ cup lemon juice*
- *1 teaspoon vegetable oil*
- *½ teaspoon garlic powder*
- *½ teaspoon red chili powder*
- *¼ teaspoon ground turmeric*
- *¼ teaspoon fresh ginger, minced*

Crab Filling

- *5 ounces crabmeat*
- *4 teaspoons vegetable oil*
- *3 cloves garlic, minced*
- *⅓ cup minced onion*
- *2 ½ teaspoons fresh ginger, minced*
- *1 tablespoon coconut milk*
- *½ teaspoon lime juice*
- *1 tablespoon cilantro, chopped*

SERVES 2

Make the Phyllo Squares

Preheat the oven to 255° F

Combine the clarified butter or ghee, turmeric, optional carom seed in a small saucepan and heat over low heat until combined for 1 to 2 minutes. Using a pastry brush, apply the butter mixture to the phyllo pastry. Using a ruler and sharp knife, cut into 3-inch squares. Put the squares on a cookie sheet lined with parchment paper. Bake for 10 minutes or until crisp.

Marinate the prawns or shrimp or crayfish.

In a small to medium bowl combine the shellfish with the yoghurt, lemon juice, garlic powder, chili powder, ginger and turmeric. Let marinate for 30 minutes.

Make the crab filling.

Thaw the crabmeat if frozen. Heat the oil in a medium sauté pan until hot but not smoking. Add the garlic, onion and ginger. Sauté until golden, 5 to 7 minutes.

Make the curry filling and combine with the crab.

Combine all the curry mixture ingredients into a small bowl.

Add 1 teaspoon of curry mixture to the garlic, onion and ginger and continue to cook for 1 to 2 minutes longer.

Add the coconut milk and stir until well-blended and most of the moisture has evaporated.

Add the crabmeat and lime juice and heat through. Remove from heat and reserve.

Cook the marinated prawns or shrimp or crayfish

Place small sauté pan over high heat. Add oil and sauté 3 to 5 minutes depending on size of shellfish. Remove the shellfish from

Courtesy of Varq

Curry Mixture for Crab Filling

- ½ teaspoon ground turmeric
- ½ teaspoon yellow chili powder
- ¾ teaspoon curry powder
- ½ teaspoon garam marsala
- ½ teaspoon freshly-ground black pepper
- Salt to taste

Garnish

- 1 chive bud or whole chive
- 1 sprig Cilantro

the pan and reserve for assembly.

Assembly

Place 1 3-inch phyllo square on a small plate. Top with 1 heaping tablespoon of crab mixture, place another phyllo square on top and another tablespoon of crab mixture on the square. Repeat until you have three layers.

Take 1 shell fish and place it on the top phyllo layer. Decorate with chive and cilantro. Repeat for the next portion.

This recipe, graciously provided by Varq, was adapted for the home cook by Cooking by the Book in New York, NY.

NOTE: To clarify butter, place it in a medium saucepan over low heat. Allow the butter to melt and then continue cooking until the foam disappears from the top and a light brown sediment forms on the bottom of the pan. When cool, the melted butter will be a clear, golden yellow.

KARIM'S – #33

The Mughals are long gone from Delhi but the rich, spicy Mughlai cuisine is alive and well at Karim's; revered in the city. It has been around since 1913 and to this day is owned by the Zahuruddin family who started it.

An ancestor of the present proprietor cooked for the Mughal emperors at court until the Mutiny of 1857, which brought an end to the Mughal rule. Realizing that a good recipe in the hand is worth two in a mutiny, he escaped with his recipes to a safer place called exile. After many years when things had calmed down, Karim's was opened in Delhi. Today prince and (relative) pauper alike show up to pay homage to the Zahuruddins.

Don't bother to look for exotic décor or relaxed dining at Karim's. The rooms are drab and stuffy. There's almost always a wait for tables, and the staff has all the courtesy of nurses in an emergency room. The story here is to get in, get out, and in between, have some of the finer grilled meats in Delhi.

Karim's is a temple where card-carrying carnivores come to worship and devour the offerings, especially the tandoori chicken. The curries here are creamy and mild in the Mughal fashion, flavored with fruits and almond paste. The one I tried was Badam Pasanda, an extravagant combination made with, among other things, lamb, yoghurt, figs and nuts. The Mughals may be long gone but their culinary memories linger delectably at Karim's.

KARIM'S/ 16 GALA KABABIAN/ JAMA MASJID/
TEL: 11-2326-9880
Moderate

 ## KARIM'S MILIEU

In my opinion, there is only one choice to be considered in the area. You're just a short walk from the largest mosque in Delhi, the Jama Masjid (pictured on page 114-115). It was built in 1656 of white marble and sandstone. Jama Masjid is a truly magnificent structure and should not be missed. There's also a small flea market at the side of the mosque and while you won't find Aladdin's lamp (at least I didn't), there are loads of trinkets that will make wonderful gifts.

MASALA ART – #34

This sleek, stylish restaurant in the Taj Palace Hotel combines contemporary Indian cuisine with the more familiar Indian menu to create an exceptional dining experience. Light woods and simple décor mirror the food here so that nothing overshadows the wonderfully inventive choices that come from Masala Art's open kitchen.

As the restaurant's name suggests, the menu is arranged with an eye to the "art" of fine Indian dining. The first page is headed by the title, "Water Colors," under which broths and soups are listed. Next is "First Impressions" for first courses, followed by "Heavy Strokes" for mains and "Final Touches" for desserts.

At Masala Art, a bread grill is rolled to your table. I watched my *chapati* being created as I started on a plate of jumbo prawns spiced with cardamom seeds. Then, still keeping an eagle eye on the progress of my *chapati*, a handsome sea bass marinated with a mint chutney was brought to the table and served with *khatti dal*, very spicy lentils, calmed by slivers of fresh, sweet mango. My *chapatti* was finally ready and more than worth the wait. My "Final Touch" was a delicate cottage cheese dumpling, enrobed in a sauce made

Courtesy of Masala Art

Jumbo Prawns

from sweetened milk.

Masala Art is the best of the past and present, blended artfully together.

Masala Art/ Taj Palace Hotel/ 2 Sardar Patel Marg/ Diplomatic Enclave/ Tel: 11-2611-0202

Moderate

MASALA ART'S MILIEU

Because the restaurant and the hotel are right in the middle of the consular community in Delhi, there's not much to see except embassies. A better plan is to hop into a cab, and head for Chandni Chowk, a fantastic bazaar in Old Delhi. The area, usually open until the wee hours, is made up of winding streets, each crammed with shops and carts and hawkers (aggressive vendors who never take "no" for an answer). The bazaar will boggle your mind and, if you're not careful, your wallet. You'll be tempted to return again and again, that is, if you're as addicted to a bargain as I am.

THE SPICE ROUTE – #35

This fabulous setting is not only a restaurant but also a geography lesson. Its mission-statement is to highlight foods that celebrate a spice route from Indonesia north to Vietnam, then east to Thailand, south to Malaysia and across the Bay of Bengal to Sri Lanka before traveling up the Malabar coast to Kerala.

The pan-Asian room has been designed to look like the inside of a temple with hand-painted murals that illustrate the stops along its culinary road. Teak columns punctuate the space and add

to the exotic atmosphere. Actually, The Spice Route looks more like a set for Indiana Jones than a restaurant in Delhi.

Because The Spice Route reflects so many different locales and cuisines, the huge menu can be a bit daunting. However, a true epicure steps up to a culinary challenge. I plowed in and started with a pungent tomato soup made with chicken and delicately flavored with coconut milk and kaffir leaves. Then onto the next stop: a Thai-style lobster sautéed with black mushrooms and ginger, and fragrant with coriander. I also tasted a mild and creamy curry from Sri Lanka, very different from the ones the some-like-it-hot crowd dotes on.

I felt I'd hardly made a dent in exploring all the areas represented on the menu but I knew I had to leave room for the *sagu sagu*, a Thai rice pudding, aromatic with a blend of cardamom and cinnamon. I finally reached the end of the road, you might say, with a few sips of pineapple *rasam*, a spicy Thai drink made with fresh curry leaves, and said to be a natural digestive. Just in the nick of time!

THE SPICE ROUTE/ THE IMPERIAL HOTEL/
JANPATH 110001/ TEL: 11-5111-6634
Expensive

THE SPICE ROUTE'S MILIEU

Once again, you'll find yourself only a hop skip and a sari away from Connaught Place. Since I suggested that you visit the area after dinner at Varq, you may feel you've been there, done that, but in truth Connaught Place is a vast area. You probably only scratched its very proper surface. This time you might like to shop for Indian crafts or fabrics to bring home. One of the best and most trustworthy places for both crafts and textiles is Cottage Industries. There are several branches of Cottage Industries in Delhi, and one of them is not far from Connaught's main shopping area. Have a look. It's usually open well past the dinner hour.

Cottage Industries/ Janpath/ Area of Delhi/ 11-2334-1234

CHOR BIZARRE – #36

No, no, I haven't spelled "bazaar" wrong. It's just that the owner of Chor Bizarre thought that it would be really terrific to make the name of the restaurant into a pun. And he never could have

gotten away with it if Chor Bizarre hadn't been such an instant culinary winner.

Chor Bazaar in India means "Thieves Market," usually a bazaar set up to sell stolen goods. But the use of the word bizarre rather than bazaar to describe the restaurant is, albeit confusing, right on the mark.

Chor Bizarre gives the word "funky" new meaning. The restaurant is crammed to the ceiling with all manner of flotsam, not to mention jetsam. Whimsically, or bizarrely, take your pick. One of the tables is made from a maharaja's bed; another from an antique sewing machine. Inviting dishes are displayed atop an antique car. It's hard to find two tables alike. Advertising art, general flea market clutter and a winding staircase that ascends to nowhere complete the scene. You would think with all the kitsch and tchotchkes

vying for your attention, the food would take a back seat. Not true.

continued on page 128

 # Chor Bizarre's Goshtaba

- *2 pounds (fatty) lamb*
- *1 cup ghee or clarified butter*
- *16 ounces whole-milk plain yoghurt*
- *2 cups milk*
- *¼ teaspoon asafetida (optional)*
- *5 small green cardamom seeds*
- *2½ tablespoons fennel powder (You may need to grind seeds to have this spice in powder form.)*
- *1 tablespoon ginger powder*
- *1 bay leaf*
- *4 cloves*
- *1-inch piece cinnamon stick*
- *2 teaspoons salt*

- *2 teaspoons dried mint for garnish*

SERVES 4 OR 5

Clean and trim meat, keeping the fat but discarding sinew. Pound meat and fat until a smooth paste is formed.

Divide meat-paste into ten portions and shape each into a ball.

For gravy, heat ghee to smoking point and then add asafoetida (if using) and yoghurt.

Cook gravy mixture till it starts bubbling. Add milk, salt, bay leaf and rest of spices. Cook on a low flame. Stir continuously to prevent the milk from curdling.

Add meatballs to the gravy and cook till they swell and are spongy. Remove bay leaf from the gravy.

Garnish meatballs with dried mint and serve hot. Tastes best when served with rice.

—Recipe by chef Rajiv Kumar Malhotra

Chor Bizarre is famous in Delhi for its excellent Kashmiri food, which is not as well known as some other cuisines in Dehli town. Because the climate in Kashmir is a bit cooler than the rest of India, the food tends to be hearty but less dependent on the use of hot chilies. One of the Kashmiri dishes that I sampled was *goshtaba*, delicate Kashmiri meatballs made from lamb and simmered in thick yoghurt scented with cardamom. Deep-fried lotus root is another Kashmiri favorite, and even though it was crisp and had a definite crunch, there was a delicacy to it. The traditional way to end a meal in Kashmir is with green tea brewed with cardamom and cinnamon, then sprinkled with chopped almonds. It was the perfect ending to a deliciously bizarre evening.

CHOR BIZARRE/ HOTEL BROADWAY/ 4-15A/
  ASAF ALI ROAD/ TEL: 11-2327-3821
Moderate

CHOR BIZARRE'S MILIEU

The location of the restaurant is between central and old Delhi. This might be a perfect time to explore the oldest part of the city. Try to make arrangments with a guide to pick you up at the restaurant or ask at Chor Bizarre for a recommendation. If you have a guide with you, exploring the bazaar, even in the early evening, should be fine—just stay alert.. A word to the wise: never agree to hire a guide who approaches you on the street. This is definitely not a good thing.

New Delhi/
Front Burner

AQUA

Wall-to-wall glamour abounds at this chi-chi poolside restaurant. Aqua boasts an enormous glass mosaic wall with a bold, abstract design in shades of blue, gray and orange. At night the pool has an aqua glow, making the small private dining areas that encircle it even more dramatic.

At Aqua, lighting is everything. As of now it's *the* place to see and be seen in Delhi.

AQUA / THE PARK HOTEL/ BANGALORE-CHENNAI/ TEL: 11-2374-3000

THE GREAT KEBAB FACTORY

The original Great Kebab Factory was located in the Radisson Hotel, and proved to be such a hit that its owners opened another to satisfy their numerous fans. Whichever branch you decide on, you'll find, as you might imagine, a kebab lover's heaven.

The glassed-in kitchen lets you watch the toothsome little darlings being made before you decide which kebabs to choose. You get four or five to an order, accompanied by four or five different *rotis* (flatbreads). Try not to eat for a month or so before visiting TGKF, just to be on the safe side.

THE GREAT KABAB FACTORY/ ANSALS FORTUNE ARCADE/ SECTOR 18, NOIDA/ TEL: 91-45-15882

An Island City-State

BEING A CREATURE OF UNCONDITIONAL habit and unable to accommodate even the slightest change in his personal itinerary, Phileas was persuaded in Singapore to temper his inflexibility to fit an adventurous twist and turn of his journey. Not that anyone would ever suggest that Fogg was becoming a devil-may-care kind of guy. Still, when the lovely Aouda, (a.k.a, the widow of the Rajah of Bunbelcund) whom he had rescued from the Rajah's funeral pyre, expressed a desire to see a bit more of Singapore, he actually agreed. It was clear he finally had found someone other than himself he desired to please.

And so, miracle of miracles, he used the interval before The Rangoon sailed on to Hong Kong to take Aouda out for a bit of quality sightseeing. Could Cupid's arrow have lodged in Fogg's carpetbag?

Jules Verne notes that Phileas "took little notice of what he saw" as he and Aouda toured Singapore. I, for one, find that hard to fathom since I had a completely different response. I found this island a sensational place to visit.

Today, if you blink, immaculate Singapore will have changed, grown and become even more successful. Because of its high energy profile, the island is a hub

continued on page 132

for commerce and technology, but part two of its story is Singapore has some of the best food in Asia.

Geographically, like Manhattan and perhaps, Alcatraz in the old days, Singapore is an island universe unto itself. It's also the smallest nation in Southeast Asia. Singaporeans call their home Singa Pura or Lion City. (I've lobbied long and hard for a change to Lyons City but so far I've been rudely rebuffed.).

When Thomas Stamford Bingley Raffles dropped anchor in Singa Pura, back in 1819, all he found were a few scattered fishing villages and a very apprehensive group of fisherman. How could he have known that his surname would someday become synonymous with first, a great bar and then a huge hotel chain? He was under the impression that he was an explorer, not an entrepreneur.

Stamford Raffles was the first to see the potential in this feisty little island, which much later would become the republic of Singapore. Today, it thrives as a major port, an oil-refining hub and as a major financial center. Although Singapore must import much of what it needs for its day-to-day existence, it handily pays for this as it grows people, skyscrapers and its industrial reputation. Singapore's less favorable face comes from the government's obsessive need to control every aspect of the people's quality of life. Its ever-vigilant government keeps Singapore on a super

tight leash—the city is one of the most tightly-supervised locales of Asia.

Law and Order is more than just a TV series on the island. If you're foolhardy enough to drop a candy wrapper on the streets of Singapore, you'll be gifted with a hefty summons. Jaywalking is completely out of the question and will earn you a stiff fine or worse, a striped suit. You may huff and puff about personal freedoms etc. but the result of this authoritarian way of life is that Singapore is one of the world's cleanest and safest cities. Though its residents might take a somewhat different view, I never, in my wanderings throughout the city, felt that I was in a "police state." As a New Yorker used to a subway system where a common diversion is watching rats foraging on the train tracks, and where trash is part of the urban scene, I can feel only astonishment at Singapore's spotless streetscape.

Often called "instant Asia," Singapore is a blend of contrasting cultures, sights and sensibilities. There's a sizable Chinatown, a Little India, an extensive Arab Street as well as a flourishing Indonesian neighborhood. Added to all of these diverse ethnic influences is its unique *Nonya* community, where Chinese and Malay populations blend.

You might say that Singapore's national cuisine is Variety. At almost any hour of the day or night,

continued on page 134

A statue of Stamford Raffles endures in the new Singapore.

you can have dim sum, snake soup, Rangoon curry or a comforting bowl of couscous. And in the unlikely event that you're not hungry, you can always go shopping for batiks, temple carvings, made-to-measure clothes, Chinese scrolls or really cheap electronics.

Orchid Road is the place for serious shoppers in Singapore. Both sides are lined with multi-level shopping malls and boutiques. I myself have spent many happy hours there, in search of the perfect silk jacket or the most colorful batiks. If you suffer from insomnia then head for the Thieves Markets (not a place to buy thieves but a heaven-on-earth for world-class bargainers). It's open until the wee hours. The Thieves Market is also famous for its street food dished out 24/7. There's no doubt about it, Singapore gives new meaning to the word diversity. In the lingua franca of the times, you could say this small island really rocks.

It's true that some of the best food in Asia can be found *in* Singapore's countless restaurants but, on the other hand, some of the best food on the island isn't found *inside* at all.

Alfresco dining in Singapore has been raised to an art form. Government licensed and government inspected (not a common practice in Asia) food stalls called "hawker centres" are everywhere. Given its overpowering need to control everything, even the island's snacks, the government decided to give the food hawkers permanent locations and watch them, you guessed it, like a hawk. Not to be confused with the snack stalls and sidewalk grills that are found on the streets of India and China, and are sometimes of questionable provenance, the stalls at the hawker centers are mini-kitchens turning out first class fare.

Diners stroll around and watch the cooks at work before making their final choices. When you finally make your selections, the waiter of your stall will deliver dinner to your numbered table. Language is not a problem; every waiter has a bit of menu-English so you can just sit back and wait for your goodies to arrive. At night, the centers are lit with colored lights; it's as if you're attending a never ending festival.

Between the outdoor food extravaganzas and the indoor elegance of its restaurants, it has always been a pleasure to Singapore for my supper.

Chili Crabs – Singapore's star specialty

THE PALM BEACH PARKING LOT – #37

The meal that I remember with the most delight when I think of Singapore wasn't eaten in a restaurant and it wasn't eaten at a hawker centre, it was devoured in a parking lot. Yes, that's what I said, a parking lot. Now, I should explain that the Palm Beach parking lot is about as far from Le Cirque as you can get. I'm not even sure that the parking lot is still there, since the last time I visited Singapore things were being demolished as quickly as they were being erected.

Located on East Coast Road, the Palm Beach parking lot accommodated both people and cars. The section of the lot where I had this unforgettable meal was a scene of utter mass confusion. Crowds of impatient diners waited for tables and waiters rushed back and forth, balancing enough plates to work for Ringling Brothers. Children and pets played under the rickety wooden tables and all the while everyone was trying to get everyone else's attention—but rarely succeeding.

If you find my (or your own) Palm Beach parking lot, you'll need to pull up a worn wooden stool, and ignore dirty dishes or icky spots on the table. The next order of business will be to flag down a waiter. This might take a certain amount of perseverance in the art of eye contact. When you finally attain your goal, order as many drinks as you think you'll need to complete your meal and a large order of Chili Crabs. The crabs are first sautéed lightly so that they remain tender and moist, heaped high on a plate and then covered with a blistering chili sauce. A thick slab of fried bread helps to savor the very last drop of spectacular sauce. Because you may never see your waiter again, except when he drops off the bill, it might be wise to add prawns in black bean sauce and the sweet and sour fish to your order, just in case.

You may ask why I'm suggesting you seek out a place that seems to resemble a war zone rather than a setting for dinner. The reason is really simple. By the time you leave your Palm Beach parking lot, you and whatever you're wearing will have experienced the best Chili Crab in all of Singapore if not the world.

The Palm Beach/ East Coast Road or ask
    a local for the best Chili Crabs/ Tel:
    Don't be silly!
Cheap!

RAFFLES HOTEL/ THE LONG BAR/ THE RAFFLES GRILL – #38 & #39

Raffles Hotel, was named for, you guessed it, Stamford Raffles, the founder of the city of Singapore. When I think of Raffles it always conjures up visions of handsome men in tropical whites, beautiful women in diaphanous chiffons, lots of bamboo furniture, palms swaying in the breeze, the whirring of ceiling fans and, most of all, intrigue.

Raffles, built in 1887 in a very proper British colonial style, operated in very British colonial

manner: no Asians were allowed inside. Amazing but true. No native Singaporean was permitted to cross its threshold as a guest until the 1930s. However, Raffles brought a kind of glamour to Singapore that only Noel Coward could have imagined.

So many legends have grown up around the Raffles through the years that the hotel has achieved its own folklore. One of the more outrageous legends is of a crazed tiger that escaped from a passing circus and was finally cornered and shot in the Raffles' billiard room. However, what is not a legend, just a sad truth, is the hotel's fate during World War II. On the eve of the Japanese invasion, many of the people who loved the Raffles gathered there for one last waltz. They knew that the enemy was getting closer and their lives would change drastically. During the Japanese occupation of Singapore, Raffles was little more than a place to billet troops. Worse, by the end of the occupation, the hotel served as a holding center for Japanese prisoners of war.

THE LONG BAR AT RAFFLES HOTEL

Almost as famous as the hotel itself, Raffles' Long Bar always has attracted a renowned following from all over the world. On the very day it opened, it became *the* place to be in Singapore.

Somerset Maugham was addicted to the Raffles' bar and could be seen during the '20s in his white linen suit, regaling all around him.

Rudyard Kipling, Noel Coward, Jean Harlow and Madonna have ordered the Long Bar's most famous concoction, the Singapore Sling. The drink is a lethal combination of everything with the possible exception of battery acid. It was created by bartender Ngiam Tong Boon in 1915, give or take. A great secret has been made of the ingredients. The original list was lost during World War II, the current one is kept locked in a safe. How "show biz" is that!

The Long Bar's decor plays right into its mystique. Done in the style of a '20s Malayan plantation, its ceiling soars to an impressive height. The room is filled with towering banana plants, palms of all varieties, wicker furniture and burnished wood. Whenever I've stopped at the Long Bar for a you-know-what, I always feel like a character right out of a '30s movie. The Long Bar is its own time machine. Where is Humphrey Bogart when you need him?

THE LONG BAR/RAFFLES HOTEL / TEL: 6412-1816
Moderate

RAFFLES GRILL

Truth be told, the Grill, revamped in the '90s, is not quite as atmospheric as the rest of Raffles. Starched white table cloths and high back chairs, not swaying palms, signal to some the formality that accompanies fine food. I must say that my dinner of Chili Crabs in the Palm Beach parking lot was as serious a meal as I've had anywhere, but the Grill Room wants your complete attention. And it deserves it because its menu more than makes up for any missing ambience. Though exotic is not a word that comes to mind here, tempting does.

Everything that would be found in most grill rooms, such as roast beef and rack of lamb, is laid out on the trolley. A carving pro lovingly slices your selection to order, solo or in combination. What isn't usually found in a restaurant dedicated to prime cuts is Suckling Pig, which was lacquered to a deep mahogany before it appeared on my plate. This little piggy was a stunner and not to be missed. A "degustation" or tasting menu gives the chef a chance to trot out all his favorites and hope that they become yours as well. If you shock easily I would advise you not to look at the right side of the menu without taking a Xanax first.

THE GRILL ROOM/ TEL: 6412-1816
Expensive and Beyond

 # Singapore Sling

A slightly less top-secret recipe

- *2 ounces (8 parts) Gin*
- *1 ounce (4 parts) cherry brandy*
- *¼ ounce (1 part) Cointreau*
- *¼ ounce (1 part) Bénédictine*
- *½ ounce (2 parts) Grenadine*
- *4 ounces (16 parts) Pineapple juice*
- *1 ½ ounces (6 parts) Fresh lemon juice*
- *1 dash Angostura bitters*
- *Pinapple for garnish*
- *Maraschino cherry for garnish*

Pour all ingredients into cocktail shaker filled with ice cubes. Shake well. Strain into Poco Grande glass. Garnish with pineapple and maraschino cherry.

Photo by Chang'r

An authentic Singapore Sling in its authentic place

 # THE GRILL ROOM'S MILIEU

The best thing to do after dinner at the Raffles Grill is to have an after dinner liqueur or an espresso along with a large helping of atmosphere in the Raffles' lush tropical courtyard. Just watching the passing parade stroll under those colonial arches in the gardens is to imagine what the Raffles Hotel must have really been like when Somerset Maugham, white linen suit and all, was seated at the next table.

LAU PA SAT HAWKER CENTRE – #40

Lau Pa Sat, almost always packed with both hungry locals and tourists, is the oldest and one of the livelier hawker centres on the island. It's a perfect place for lunch when you visit the nearby Singapore Handicrafts Centre.

"Lau Pa" means "Old Market," and its central umbrella is a graceful Victorian octagon. Unlike most of the other centres, much of its seating is indoors. Lau Pa Sat was designated a national monument in the '70s.

Food stalls line the octogon's edges and offer

 LAU PA SAT'S MILIEU

After lunch or dinner wander over to the Singapore Handicraft Centre. It's not far from Lau Pa. There are always demonstrations to watch, if not batik design then in weaving or leather craft. Be forewarned, the demos exist to prime the pump for a purchase or two.

Courtesy of Singapore Tourism Board

seemingly endless choices. Each vendor specializes in one or a few. Possible selections include pork Satay perfumed with coriander and cumin, crisp onion pancakes. vegetable crepes, crunchy Indian chicken deep fried to a golden crunch then doused with a fiery chili sauce and Chinese barbequed meats rubbed with spices and chilies. You'll also see baskets of quivering crustaceans waiting to be part of what seems to be Singapore's national dish, Chili Crab. Chili sauce is to Singapore what ketchup is to Coney Island.

If you decide against beer or Diet Coke, you can order a spectacularly sweet libation found everywhere on the island. It's known as fresh lychee juice. I can't really describe how they go about juicing a lychee but the result is pure heaven.

LAU PA SAT FOOD CENTRE/ CORNER OF BOON TAT STREET/ OPEN DAILY FROM NOON TO 10P.M.
Inexpensive

CHEN FU JI SING'S SENSATION – #41

Astonishing but true is the average Singaporean's unending devotion to that universal of all Asian side dishes: fried rice. Who knew? Mind you, this is not quite the same fried rice that most westerners stopped ordering once they'd passed their seventh birthdays. Singapore cooks have raised the profile of this simple dish to a mini art-form. One of the better places to sample phenomenal fried rice is Chen Fu Ji, founded by the Chen sisters over 50 years ago. There are several different branches but my favorite is known as Chen Fu Ji Sing's Sensation.

Sing's Sensation overlooks the Singapore River and has floor-to-ceiling windows to capture the view. The menu here is seriously devoted to making Chen's pampered kernels into five-star generals. The fried rice that Chen's serves is either crowned with a halo of fresh crabmeat or sautéed tiger prawns or smoked duck. The most popular dish of all, especially with the regulars, is Imperial Fried Rice which features sautéed crabmeat and stir-fried eggs.

CHEN FU JI'S MILIEU

Take the waterfront walk opposite Chen Fu Ji's, to see Singapore's wonderfully multicultural society in action. And it doesn't matter how late the hour--- remember this is Singapore, everybody's watching everybody else.

Chen Fu Ji also has its own take on fusion cuisine. A cook carefully molds warm fried rice into a cake and then couples it with ice cream. I'd say that it's a triumph of yin versus yang. I know the combination sounds a bit schizophrenic but it has become the "Chubby Hubby" (Ben and Jerry take note) of Singapore.

CHEN FU JI SING'S SENSATION
30 MERCHANT'S ROAD/ RIVERSIDE POINT/ TEL: 653-301-66
Inexpensive

Singapore/
Front Burner

BLU

BLU, under chef, Kevin Cherkas, is considered one of the elegant newer dining spots in Singapore. Perched on the 24th floor of the Shangri-La hotel, it has accents by none other than Phillip Starke. Having schlepped his star studded Michelin reputation all the way from Spain, France and Kuala Lampur, Kevin is certainly stirring up foodies. It's only a matter of time before he adds another twinkler to his belt at his newest outpost.

BLU/ 22 ORANGE GROVE ROAD/ SHANGRI-LA HOTEL/ TEL # 6737-3644

INDOCHINE WATERFRONT

A recent entry serving Vietnamese cuisine has charmed much of the island's population. The dishes served echo Vietnam's colonial past. True to its name, it has lovely views of the water.

INDOCHINE WATERFRONT/ 1 EMPRESS PLACE/ ASIAN CIVILIZATIONS MUSEUM/ TEL: 65-6339-1720

Taipei/
Detour

I CAN NEVER VISIT THE FAR EAST without a small helping of Taipei on my agenda. It's a destination that has been overlooked by many, including Phileas Fogg, or treated as just a whistle-stop on the way to the far more glamourous Hong Kong or Singapore. Well, although Tapei may be a detour from Fogg's route, don't you believe that it is not worth your time. Taiwan's capital city is, in reality, the capital of Chinese food. Among those who fled China after Mao's takeover were many fine cooks from every mainland province. This particular migration disproved the adage that too many cooks spoil the egg drop soup. On the contrary, not only did the soup improve because of these regional masters but dining in Taipei became an adventure in diversity. Within the city limits there is a culinary empire made up of all of the great cuisines of China. On any given day, the best of Shanghai, Beijing and Hong Kong as well as the provinces of Sichuan, Fukien and Hunan, are served up with enormous pride. You could call it a culinary national anthem.

Taiwan was once known as *Ilha Formosa*, the Portuguese name for "beautiful island." The Portuguese were inspired to name it that in 1544 when they discovered it. The Dutch, in 1624, found it even more attractive and claimed it as a new colony.

For a relatively small island Taipei has suffered through massive upheaval and conflict. The name Formosa rings a bell with people of a certain age since Formosa was a major World War II battle site. The Japanese who had staked their claim on the island in 1859 found it to be an essential

continued on page 146

staging area for operations by its navy during the Second World War. Formosa sustained heavy and repeated bombing by the American Forces. After the war, the island was made part of China. Formosa became Taiwan when the Chinese nationalists took over in 1949.

The Taipei of today is nothing like sophisticated and stylish Hong Kong. It's much plainer and more dependable, like a slightly frumpy aunt that you can always count on for a quick hug and a slice of chocolate cake. As far as natural beauty is concerned, Taipei may come up a bit short compared to some Asian neighbors.

Through the years, Taiwan has become a symbol of political resistance and a commercial force, excelling in computer technology. Even as we speak, a more liberal China is making every effort to give Taiwan a big panda hug to entice it back into the fold. Taiwan has signaled that it just might be open to some lucrative persuasion. Stayed tuned.

DIN TAI FUNG – #42

Din Tai Fung long has been on my radar screen, and recently, *Time* magazine seems to have discovered it as well. *Time* rated it "one of the 10 best restaurants in the world." Now that may be pushing the envelope just a bit, but there's no denying that Din's soup dumplings, those devilish little mouthfuls with a liquid surprise, would be on anyone's short list for terrific and that explains the mob outside this bare bones store. So much for that little place no one knows about yet.

A window which is perpetually steamed up and a big red sign with Chinese lettering mark the spot for Din. Hang in there, the long wait gives you time to sneak a peek at others' plates and fantasize about actually getting something to eat.

There are many choices on the menu aside from soup dumplings. Prawns done in a tart orange sauce or baked spare ribs and pork chops, for instance, but nothing even comes close to the delight of biting down ever so gently on those little pillows of tender dough and then savoring the rush of tasty broth that follows.

DIN TAI FUNG/ 194 XIN YI ROAD/ TEL: 02-2391-7719
Moderate

🎈 DIN TAI FUNG'S MILIEU

As with most of Taipei, everything is just a short walk or an inexpensive cab drive away. And so planning a trip to the National Palace Museum is a cinch. But after all of those soup dumplings, perhaps the best revenge is brisk exercise as well as some even brisker shopping to get you ready for your midnight snack.

YONGHE SOY MILK KING – #43

My guess would have been that if one is referred to as the king of soy milk, not only is he a health food colossus but also someone who knows firsthand the meaning of "lactose intolerant."

Not in Taipei. Soy milk shops are the equivalent of stateside Dairy Queens. Everyone gathers there for a quick pick-me-up with any number of soy milk concoctions made with either black or white soy milk and served hot or cold. I found that one of the more satisfying breakfasts in the city is a chilled glass of soy milk accompanied by a pair of deep-fried crullers. I know, I know, all the benefits of the soy milk are instantly cancelled out by the killer-crullers. But in Taipei, you're often faced with the yin and yang of the Chinese kitchen, crullers and all.

YONGHE SOY MILK KING/ 132 FU XING SOUTH
ROAD, SECTION 2/ 02-2702-1226
Inexpensive

YONGHE'S MILIEU

Yonghe is open 24 hours a day and filled with Xing South Road shoppers. The shops are also open late. Yonghe, by far the best of many soy milk shops on South Road, is a favorite destination. The area is packed solid with young, hip Taiwainese during the wee hours. You can stop in for a late or early breakfast, a light lunch or a quick snack, pre or post shopping. With all those options, how can you go wrong?

PENG YUAN – #44

If I had time for only one meal (horrors) in Taipei, I would choose to have it at Peng Yuan. It has long been the darling of the kitchen gods as well as most of the population. When I was last there, chef Peng Chang Gui was uncertain about his future (I guess we could all say that).

But my meal there was well worth remembering as well as repeating as often as possible, and I'm keeping my chopsticks crossed. In the event that Peng finally has closed his doors, he can rejoice in the knowledge that his government has formally recognized him as a National Treasure.

Photo by Aiki-dude

The word around town is that to be taken seriously as a chef in Taipei, you had to make your bones, quite literally, with chef Peng. The dish that he's best known for is a sybaritic Hunanese mixture of thick slices of smoked ham soaked in golden honey and then pressed between two slices of fresh-baked white bread. You could call it the world's most brilliant ham sandwich. Peng's other showstopper is a giant scallop, delicately steamed in its own bamboo cup and then drizzled with a rich-as-Bloomberg fish broth. You can bet your last water chestnut that in a city where the restaurant scene is taken almost as seriously as the Taiwanese Stock Market, Peng Yuan has money in the bank.

Peng Yang/ 380 Linshen North Road/ Tel: Unlisted, no reservations accepted or required
Moderate

PEN YUAN'S MILIEU

Perhaps not right next door, but close enough with a short cab ride, is one of the most hiss-toric sights in the city: Snake Alley. This is home base for Asian health food addicts as well as a herpetologist or two. The street is lined with storefront restaurants adorned with cages filled with slithering sweeties who have limited futures. All the patron has to do is point to a cooperative cobra or a bashful boa and the maitre d' will fillet the live reptile of choice before the diner's very eyes. Sad to say, as I watched, what came to mind was a glorious vision of shoes. Before you can say snakeskin Manolos the meat has been thrown into a pot and simmered to make a hearty, good-for-what-ails-you Snake Soup. Campbell's, take note. Most Chinese believe that snake soup is not only a restorative but can be used as a jump start in the toujours l'amour *department. Apparently Viagra will never replace a really delicious reptile in the hearts of the Taiwanese.*

Snake Alley is also known as Huashi Street, but that's no fun.

Author's disclaimer: Snake Alley is not one of the recommended dining spots for the reader. This experience, while it may be sharper than a serpent's tooth, is meant for viewing, not dining. Those who simply can't resist a viper in a bowl, indulge at their own risk.

TEA AT THE GRAND HOTEL – #45

Not the best British Tea in Taipei, but not the worst either. It really doesn't matter, whatever excuse you use to visit the Grand Hotel is worth it.

One of the visual wonders of Taipei, though no longer considered to be one of Taipei's five-star hotels, the Grand is a magnificent structure. Perched on the top of a hill, it can be seen from almost anywhere in Taipei, like a monumental temple and almost as startling to come upon as Shangri La. The Grand's public rooms are vast as well as extraordinary. From any of the terraces the views of the city below are sensational.

After Chiang Kai-Shek left mainland China, he needed an appropriate setting to entertain ambassadors and diplomats as well as an appropriate place to hold state functions. The Grand was opened in 1952 and was considered a magnificent, world class hotel. It became Chiang's official diplomatic residence. The President and Madam Chiang Kai-Shek often stayed in the Grand's Presidential Suite, which today can be reserved by anyone who has $4,850 to spare. Each of the Grand's enormous levels (floors) is named for a different Chinese dynasty.

THE GRAND HOTEL/ 1 CHUNG SHAN ROAD
    NORTH/ TEL: 02-2886-8888
Moderate

THE GRAND HOTEL'S MILIEU

Once again you'll find yourself just a short distance from the National Palace Museum, so if you haven't had a chance to spend time there it would be a shame not to coordinate tea at the hotel with a visit.

Taipei/
Front Burner

APOCALYPSE NOW

Asian fusion, a DJ and beer on tap makes this a special spot for the young crowd in Taipei. Not for elegant dining but fun if you like beer with your egg rolls.

APOCALYPSE NOW/ 323 FUHSING NORTH ROAD/ TEL: 2-2545-4628

C'EST BON

Forget the name, *C'est Bon* is not your mother's French restaurant. In France c'est bon means "it's good" but in Taipei it means "way of eating." True to the restaurant's name, chef Ah-jiau Chuang produces some of the best eating to be seen in Taipei in years, and that's saying a lot. Her devotees line up in droves for her duck-taro and shrimp pancake as well as the other surprises that she has in store for them. They say arriving early is essential.

C'EST BON / 23 LANE 33/ CHUNG-SHANG NORTH ROAD/ TEL: 2-2531-6408

~ CHINA ~

Hong Kong

"There are about 1,300 miles between
Singapore and the island of Hong Kong . . .
Phileas Fogg needed to cover this distance in
six days, at the most."

— Jules Verne

ARRIVING AT HONG KONG ON The Rangoon almost a day late due to a storm at sea, both Phileas and Passepartout were apoplectic, to say the least. Mother Nature had taken Fogg's schedule and torn it up. The fact to be faced was that, in a falling domino fashion, he could well miss the boat booked to take him to Yokohama and therefore miss the steamer in Yokohama bound for San Francisco. At this critical moment, in all likelihood Phileas Fogg would lose his wager. To say that he was in no mood for a plate of dim sum might be stating the obvious.

In *Around the World in Eighty Days*, Verne emphasized the finite possibilities of Hong Kong: "Hong Kong is only a small island, ceded to Great Britain by the Treaty

continued on page 154

of Nanking after the war of 1842." If Verne were to visit it now, he might be struck dumb by the changes that have been accomplished since his favorite tourist, Phileas Fogg, arrived. Today, the best way to describe Hong Kong is existing in a state of perpetual motion, with a dose of steroids for good measure. Manhattan could be thought of as a ghost town next to the never-ending, round-the-clock action that makes Hong Kong the capital of very conspicuous consumption. It also rivals Tokyo for neon and Paris for chic.

For years Hong Kong has clung to the edge of a dangerously steep cliff. First, it held on for dear life as it waited for the clock to run out on British rule. Having survived the changeover, it's now in a state of suspended apprehension, nervously waiting for Beijing to put its foot down on its errant child's fun and games—in effect to put an end to everything that has made Hong Kong the Land of Oz, Asian-style. However, and to Hong Kong's immense relief, China decided, instead, to transform more compliant Shanghai into an international business powerhouse and play-land.

Almost no matter what the future holds for Hong Kong, it's likely to remain a money magnet, an irresistible metropolis for the legions of western and Chinese bankers, real estate moguls, tailors, jewelers and techies who call it home. No doubt, poverty will remain part of the Hong Kong scene.

Still, almost nothing can compete with the city's dazzling geography and manmade glitter which eclipse corners of harsher reality.

Many islands in the South China Sea and a peninsula make up what we think of as Hong Kong. Hong Kong Island, with Victoria Peak, as well as some of the city's very affluent neighborhoods, faces the peninsular tip, Kowloon, across magnificent Victoria Harbour. Kowloon is where luxury hotels add patina to Hong Kong's glamour. Not quite so flamboyant but still part of the city are the New Territories, also on the peninsula jutting from the Chinese mainland, and numerous nearby small islands in the South China Sea. Hong Kong is, in fact, a many splendored thing.

If, by some outrageous turn of fate, I had only one day to spend in Hong Kong, I'm sure that I would spend most of it riding back and forth

Photo by BrokenSphere

across Victoria Harbour on the Star ferry. To me, the ferry represents the very essence of Hong Kong. Carrying passengers between Hong Kong Island and Kowloon, a trip that takes about eight minutes, it permits the breathtaking panorama of the harbor to unfold slowly. Junks loaded with goods sail elegantly by; ancient looking sampans ferry people from shore-to-shore; small sailboats dot the water like tiny birds. It's true that there are a number of harbors around the world that are heart stopping but in Hong Kong, the harbor acts as a glorious punctuation mark to the frenzy that surrounds it.

You might say that Confucius was China's very

first food critic. He believed that food should be carefully selected in the market, specifying "no brown meat" (he obviously never had dinner on a plane), "no damp or discolored rice" and "eating in moderation." He also advised on proper table manners which meant that food should be cut into little pieces so as to not make the diner grapple with large chunks—wise words for the country which 500 years earlier had adopted chopsticks. Yet little did Confucius know that two millennia later, people in the New World would be helplessly watching food they'd tried to grasp slip slowly back onto their plates or, even worse, their clothing without ever making contact with their mouths.

Most visitors arrive in Hong Kong armed with a list of restaurants as long as the Great Wall. It's been said that it would be possible to eat at a different restaurant every day for two years in HK, and never repeat a dish. I have yet to speak to anyone who's had the time or fortitude to test that assertion, not even the Guinness boys.

The food in Hong Kong is epitomized by its dazzling array of choices, and Michelin has taken note of one great Cantonese restaurant. It has awarded three stars, its highest accolade, to Lung King Heen, under chef Chan Yan Tak at the Four Season's Hotel. The award was a special triumph for Chan since the popularity of the Cantonese kitchen, has been somewhat eclipsed by the food of other provinces such as Hunan, Sichuan and Fujian.

In Hong Kong, as in the rest of China, it really doesn't matter if it's street food or a three-star tummy temple. Through the centuries, the Chinese have had two great passions, food and gambling. Nothing has really changed, and food has the edge if ever so slightly.

LUK YU TEA HOUSE – #46

Dim sum, roughly translated means "to touch the heart." Even more important, eating dim sum in Hong Kong means to touch *its* heart. And the best place to do that is the Luk Yu Tea House. In a city where everyone plays "Beat the Clock" day and night, Luk Yu is the closest any of us will come to the memory of the old, colonial Hong Kong. Hand-carved rosewood booths, stained-glass murals, languid ceiling fans humming away and framed Chinese scrolls on the walls, it's all there. And while Luk Yu might not serve the most delicate dim sum to be found, it really doesn't matter. Luk Yu is about so much more. I was told by the manager of the Peninsula Hotel, that iconic Hong Kong landmark, that teahouses on the island were fast disappearing. Everyone who visits Hong Kong should go to Luk Yu at least once, he said, "to see how things used to be." It's easy to understand why the dedicated regulars of a certain age who start their day here create an atmosphere that's more 1890s than new millennium.

Don't bother to look for an English menu or

the usual dim sum trolleys at lunch. Don't even think of arguing when you're banished to Siberia on the third floor. The best defense is just to smile at your unsmiling waiter, and point to the plates on other tables. Midmorning is the most difficult time to snag a table.

On one of my many visits, I luk-ed out with a plate of steamed dumplings filled with liver sausage and ginger, but that was only the beginning. After multi-servings of assorted pancakes, buns, balls, puffs and other treasures from the kitchen, I was amazed to find that the teahouse actually served dessert. Usually, if dessert is served at all in a Chinese restaurant, it turns out to be a sweet bean soup, definitely no substitute

for a slice of cheesecake. So to find an elegant Twiggy-thin crepe filled with custard and fresh fruit was, indeed, an inscrutable surprise.

LUK YU TEA HOUSE/24-26 STANLEY STREET/
    TEL: 523-5464
Moderate

LUK YU'S MILIEU

Stanley Street is right off Queens Road which offers a wonderful counterpoint to the old Hong Kong of Luk Yu. Most of Queens Road is devoted to tall, glass skyscrapers and formidable banks. A case in point is the mega-modern Bank of China. However, even in this 21st century streetscape, there's a hint of yesterday. The Bank of China stands next to the Hong Kong and Shanghai Banking Corporation, which was the bank that represented the British when Hong Kong was a crown colony. There are two huge lions at its entrance that make it clear the Brits were not about to go without a roar.

CLEVELAND SZECHUAN – #47

There is simply no way to capture precisely the sights, the sounds and the smells that greet you at Cleveland Szechuan. First, you have to climb to the top of a steep flight of stairs to get a look at the huge round tables which are filled with huge round families in a generational display of dining unity. Everyone seems to be speaking at once as they reach for the multitude of platters in the center of the table. The Cleveland is known for some of the best Szechuan food in Hong Kong.

The last time I was there I had the misfortune of having only one other person with me. Understandably, a party of two is pretty puny by Cleveland's standards; still we were welcomed and seated at a table with other temporary orphans. In the end, it all worked out wonderfully well and actually led to the unexpected opportunity for even more tasting.

Some of the choices on the menu are familiar to Chinese-food lovers and have become old friends in the States. Eggplant with garlic sauce can usually be counted on to provide some heat from the chilies used in the sautéing. But at the Cleveland, this dish should be served with its own fire extinguisher. Through the years, I've found that there is no better antidote for jetlag. My personal favorites on the menu include the

CLEVELAND SZECHUAN'S MILIEU

Not far from the restaurant is Victoria Park, one of the lovelier on Hong Kong Island, a perfect place to recharge after all the noise and the confusion of the restaurant. At the entrance to the park is a statue of a seated Queen Victoria, (even she had to relax from time to time) with a somewhat intriguing past. After the Japanese invaded Hong Kong, they rounded up almost all the bronze statues and had them sent back to Japan to be melted down for the war effort. But the Queen escaped that fate. Her manners were known to be impeccable. She would never have participated in a meltdown of any kind. After the war, she was returned to Hong Kong and placed triumphantly back at the park entrance.

Photo by Jeromy-Yu Chan Arad

Golden Carp, glistening in its rich vegetable broth and perfumed with a touch of garlic, and the Camphor and Tea Duck, smoked over camphor wood, and served with steamed bread. As for the "offal" truth at the Cleveland, the adventurous can dig into such savory delights as Pig's Kidney and Stewed Beef Heart.

CLEVELAND SZECHUAN/6 CLEVELAND STREET/
CAUSEWAY BAY/ TEL: 576-3876
Moderate

THE JUMBO FLOATING RESTAURANT – #48

When I first caught sight of the Jumbo Floating Restaurant, I thought that it might have been a figment of my imagination. It sits like some nautical mirage aglow with colored lights in the middle of Aberdeen Harbour. The Jumbo has the kitsch of Disneyland, the cosmopolitan bling of New York's once great Tavern on the Green and the exotic charm of Copenhagen's Tivoli amusement park. It's a real stunner.

Now, I'll have to admit that if the Jumbo was to have been my only meal in Hong Kong I might have resisted its twinkling invitation and gone to one of the island's more venerable temples of gastronomy. But that said, don't let anyone deter you from a visit to the Jumbo because it's "just too touristy." That makes as much sense as avoiding the Eiffel Tower because you can see it on a postcard. Stand firm as I did, and just go. And stand just as firmly in *not* going to the other floating restaurants in Aberdeen. They don't even come close to the ditsy charm of the Jumbo.

After admiring the Jumbo from the shore, glittering for all its worth, you look for the thousands of signs that will lead you to the pier and then board a small, ferry marked "Jumbo." It will take you out to the middle of the bay and the Jumbo's entrance. As you get closer, though hard to believe, the Jumbo gets even brighter. Once you've stepped on deck it's clear that the lights aren't the only things that make the Jumbo unforgettable. The decor on this floating phantasma is straight out of an old Charlie Chan movie. There are more dragons than St. George could shake a sword at, more tassels than

Gypsy Rose Lee bought in her whole career, and enough gilt to make Ikea look like Versailles. The Jumbo can seat over 3000 comfortably so don't even think about intimate dining. Perhaps most delightful of all, after you've had a fairly uninspired meal you can play dress up with outfits for empress or emperor wannabes. The night I was there, a sweet, newly married couple was posing up a storm for the house photographer. You might well ask if I chose to make that much of a fool of myself. You bet your eggroll I did. And, I have the snapshot to prove it.

As for the food, after you get used to the sensory overload think neighborhood Cantonese.

But to miss the Jumbo would be to miss the quirky, off-the-wall charm of Hong Kong itself.

THE JUMBO FLOATING RESTAURANT/ ABERDEEN HARBOUR/ TEL: 553-9111
Moderate

THE JUMBO'S MILIEU

Unless you have your scuba equipment with you, don't try strolling through the harbor after dinner.

TEA AT THE PENINSULA HOTEL – #49

"The Pen," as it's called by its loyal fans, is to Hong Kong what the Savoy Hotel is to London. The Pen has been around since 1928 and it has never lost its notable status, not even when the Japanese made it their headquarters during WWII. That's the very reason the Japanese chose it. Even *they* knew it was the place to be.

Though the Pen's location is not right at the edge of the harbor, it makes up for the loss of view with its colonial elegance and gilded ceilings. Most

(continued on page 164)

Peninsula Hotel's Chive Dumplings

Dumplings

- *1 pound medium shrimp, finely minced*
- *2 tablespoons chives, minced*
- *⅓ cup Shiitake mushrooms, finely diced*
- *2 tablespoons vegetable oil*
- *1 teaspoon salt*
- *1 teaspoon sugar*

Pastry

- *5 tablespoons all purpose flour*
- *5 tablespoons cornstarch*
- *¾ cup water*

MAKES 24 3-INCH DUMPLINGS

This recipe, provided by the Peninsula Hotel, was adapted for the home cook by Cooking by the Book in New York, NY.

In a medium bowl combine the shrimp meat with the chives, mushrooms, vegetables, oil, salt and sugar. Refrigerate until ready to make the dumplings, or up to 4 hours.

To make the dumpling skins, whisk the flour and cornstarch in a small bowl. Heat the water in a small pot over medium heat. When the water comes to a simmer add the flour mixture and stir vigorously until the mixture comes together in a ball. Remove from heat and start to make your dumpling skins. Take about 1 well rounded teaspoon of dough for each dumpling and roll it out on a floured board to ⅟₃₂ of an inch. You should be able to see your finger through the skin. Place 1 to 2 teaspoons of filling on top of the skin, using your finger coat the skin perimeter with water, then press closed to make a small purse shape. Keep the completed dumplings covered with a damp towel or plastic wrap.

Place a steamer insert over simmering water and place in one layer of dumplings. Steam dumplings for 4-5 minutes. Repeat with the remaining dumplings. Serve with soy sauce.

of all, the specialty of the house is timelessness. The wicker and bamboo chairs in the lobby are filled every afternoon with American moguls, nostalgic Brits, Chinese tourists and Hong Kong "chuppies" (Chinese yuppies). They come for their daily fix of Earl Grey tea and homemade buttery scones, served with outrageously thick clotted cream. Although one can order a reputable Chinese tea with dim sum, the scene hasn't changed much since the days of the Crown Colony. Nor have the fresh-baked scones.

THE PENINSULA /SALISBURY ROAD, KOWLOON/
    TEL: 366-6251
Expensive

THE PENINSULA'S MILIEU

Salisbury Road is in the middle of luxury hotel territory, with the Peninsula, the Mandarin Oriental and the Intercontinental just steps from one another. If you have any desire to be in stitches in Hong Kong, now is the time to check out the bespoke (custom-made clothing) scene at one of the hotels. Few people leave Hong Kong without something new and silky to squeeze into their suitcases.

SPRING DEER – #50

Hong Kong has so many glitzy, ritzy and bedazzling venues for taking in sustenance that I always look forward to visiting Spring Deer. It's a vacation from the island's food-aholic chaos. It has been providing Pekinese (the city, not the dog) food for over 30 years. Today, Peking is known as Beijing.

Spring Deer is famous not only for its comfort food served up in a comfortable setting, but also

for its informality. The bad news is that I am not the only one who is aware of Spring Deer's warm welcome. In fact, the place is almost always packed with Deer's loyal fans. They know that they can get one of the best versions of Peking Duck to be found in all of Hong Kong, and at a reasonable price, too.

The preparation of Peking Duck at Spring Deer is an exercise in frugality. Traditionally, the cook uses every part of the duck except, as they say, the quack. When it is done cooking in all its mahogany splendor, the duck will glisten with a honey glaze and have skin that's crisper than a banker's shirt. The crackling skin is sliced into thin strips and served with shards of spring onion and cucumber carefully wrapped together in a steamed, paper-thin pancake. The succulent duck meat is carved off the carcass and sautéed with bean sprouts. But, there's still more to come in this ultimate Peking Duck-ology: the purist diner can request a thick custard made from the fat of the bird, much to the dismay of cardiologists all over the world. And even that is not the end of our poor, dead Donald. A double-rich stock made from the bones and scraps is turned into a duck soup that would have made the Marx Brothers weep. Be forewarned, there can be a wait of at least 45 minutes to an hour before you ever see your de-feathered friend. After all, it takes time to create a masterpiece.

Spring Deer/ 42 Mody Road, Kowloon/
    Tel: 852-2366
Moderate

SPRING DEER'S MILIEU

Mody Road is a short distance from the swank hotels of Salisbury Road as well as the ferry that goes to Discovery Bay, located at the tip of Lantau Island. If you want to get a peek at another HK island, now's your chance. Discovery Bay was a resort area with a manmade beach but now most of it is devoted to housing. What a waste.

THE LOBBY LOUNGE AT THE HOTEL INTERCONTINENTAL – #51

If a room with a view makes your heart beat faster, then a bar with a spectacular view may require a bottle of smelling salts. There's no doubt about it, the view of Victoria Harbour from the panoramic windows of the Lobby Lounge at the Intercontinental Hotel gets the prize for sheer drama. The windows offer almost 360 degrees of pure spectacle.

Sinking down into one of the super-comfortable chairs in the Lounge and sipping

Photo by Tim Olsen

one of its brilliant martinis is something that I never fail to accomplish when I'm in Hong Kong. In fact, my husband Ivan and I once spent almost six hours in the Lobby Lounge (the wait staff was really permissive) working out the plot for a new novel. Needless to say, the martinis gave the plot some extra twists, aside from the ones in the stemware.

The Lobby Lounge also serves a formal Chinese Tea in the afternoon with many varieties of green or black tea among which to choose. Try to go in the late afternoon so that you can watch the sunset, the time that the harbor is at its most seductive.

Or stop in after dark to catch the city at its sparkling best.

HOTEL INTERCONTINENTAL/ SALIBURY ROAD, KOWLOON/ 852-2721-1211
Expensive

THE PEAK LOOKOUT CAFÉ – #52

As if it weren't enough to marvel at Hong Kong's breathtaking harbor from Kowloon or Hong Kong Island, you can vary the view and look at it from above. All you have to do is take a possibly terrifying ride on the Peak Tram to the top of Victoria Peak. It's nothing but chills and thrills as the tram ascends the super- steep side of the mountain to its peak at 1,300 feet.

Upon arrival and perhaps after a call to your therapist, you can concentrate on a snack or even a simple dinner at the Peak Lookout Café.

Dating back to 1901, this charming, colonial

rest stop at the top of the peak started out as just that. In the days of British rule, coolies with rickshaws and sedan chairs were the transportation of choice for the solid-gold English colonizers who lived at the top of Victoria Mountain. They were carried back and forth, up and down and even around the mountain

Photos courtesy of the Peak Lookout Café

to their sumptuous mansions, far from the heat of the island below. The poor, overworked and underpaid schleppers as well as their schleppees needed a place to rest and a cool drink. Faster than a speeding kumquat, a simple restaurant was opened for refreshments. Of course the rules of "upstairs, downstairs" were carefully observed and "downstairs" had their drinks in each other's company.

Today after a much needed facelift, the café is one of the popular destinations in town, not only for its restorative powers but for its wondrous

THE PEAK LOOKOUT CAFÉ'S MILIEU

If you find hiking more satisfying as an exercise than martini drinking (I find that mixing a really good martini takes an overwhelming amount of muscle coordination), then you have a whole mountain at your disposal. The walk back to town gives you a chance to see some of the astounding McMansions along the way.

view. The menu is surprisingly eclectic as well as multicultural. You can order Thai spring rolls, a shellfish platter, Indian *samosas,* hamburgers and chicken quesadilla. Or you can go straight to cappuccino or dessert. If possible, try to get a table outside and then it really doesn't matter what you eat because the most exciting thing on the menu is the scenery.

THE PEAK LOOKOUT CAFÉ/ 121 PEAK ROAD/
TEL: 852-2849-1000
Moderate

THE CAUSEWAY BAY TYPHOON SHELTER – #53

You may have dreamed of taking a slow boat to China but you can compromise and take a slow boat *in* China. Have you ever dined shipboard with a starched white table cloth, crystal wine glasses, your food served by a deferential waiter? Well, no matter. You still might like to try your luck eating on a small, rolling sampan in the middle of one of Hong Kong's typhoon shelters, especially Aberdeen Harbour or Causeway Bay.

A typhoon shelter is an area set aside to shelter small fishing boats from the fierce storms that frequently descend on Hong Kong. These boats make up floating cities that are the permanent homes to hundreds of Hong Kong residents. There are people who were born, grew up, married and died

Causeway Bay Typhoon shelter at night

on their boats, never having lived on dry land.

One of the unique eating experiences in Hong Kong starts with taking a cab to the shore of one of the shelters (the shelters in Aberdeen and Causeway Bay don't have formal addresses but the

drivers all know where to drop you). Before you know it, a small sampan, one of many that wait for customers, will row over and ask if you'd like to have some food. By this time there's no turning back nor should you because both the experience and the meal will be more than worth it.

My sampan in the Causeway Bay Typhoon Shelter was rowed by a woman old enough to have known the last emperor personally. However, she handled the craft with the expertise of Christopher Columbus. The boat had room for two, not counting its captain. There was something that suggested a table but it was more like a tray that kept moving up and down with the motion of the boat. This is definitely not meant to be black-tie dining.

As we approached the shelter, my ancient mariner shouted and gestured wildly to a tiny fleet of kitchen sampans that instantly surrounded our boat, furiously preparing my dinner. I tried in

vain to mop the spray of the waves from my face, as we rowed from boat to boat but I still managed to point to a noodle dish here, a basket of fried dumplings there, until I had chosen as many courses as I thought I could manage before my dining room sank.

You could liken the cooking sampans to a convoy of floating dim sum trolleys. Each one had a different specialty. Chili crabs might be to the starboard, sautéed beans to the stern. One of the sampans even carried a tiny Chinese orchestra playing ricky-ticky tunes to chew by. Of all the food experiences in Hong Kong, this one is not to be missed. As the twilight deepens, the flames from the woks and the festive colored lanterns magically illuminate your floating dinner.

CAUSEWAY BAY TYPHOON SHELTER/
ABERDEEN TYPHOON SHELTER
Inexpensive

Aberdeen Bay

 CAUSEWAY BAY'S MILIEU

Causeway Bay is just about the smallest district in Hong Kong. Aside from its typhoon shelter, it is filled with department stores (a favorite is China Products near Paterson Street) and the ever present crush of the crowds. There are millions of small shops and food stalls to be explored after your shipboard adventure.

Causeway Bay is also famous for its Noonday Gun which used to signal the lunch hour with several cannons firing when the sun had reached its height—just so you'd know when you needed to run for cover. The Gun was immortalized by Noel Coward in his song "Mad Dogs and Englishmen."

Hong Kong/
Front Burner

LUNG KING HEEN

The address (a street called Finance) of this superb restaurant is some indication of its menu prices. Most people agree after dining at Lung King Heen, it is *so* worth it. And the inspector from Michelin agreed, as I mentioned earlier. The award not only celebrated Cantonese cuisine, it was the very first time any chef in China had triple-starred in one of its guides.

Lung King Heen means "View of the Dragon," so called because of the spectacular views of Victoria Harbour from its windows. Any self-respecting dragon would be impressed. The restaurant's Cantonese dishes are done with contemporary flare.

LUNG KING HEEN/ FOUR SEASONS HOTEL/8 FINANCE STREET, CENTRAL/ TEL: 852-3196-8888

Beijing/
Detour

The last time we looked in on Phileas, he was, metaphorically speaking, hanging from a pier by his fingernails. How would he make up the time he had lost because of that unfortunate storm at sea? Would he arrive back in London in time to win his bet? All of this might have been quite suspenseful had not dedicated readers of Jules Verne's remarkable adventure novels known that the author would never dream of leaving Phileas in such a precarious position. The intrepid Fogg would ultimately triumph over adversity and the clock.

On the other hand it might be fun to think of Fogg temporarily throwing in the towel and allowing himself to take an intriguing detour to Beijing. My guess is that if, by some miracle, he had agreed, he would not have regretted a single moment springing from his very uncharacteristic decision. Once there, Phileas would never have been able to resist the lure of the Forbidden City, which in those days was really forbidding, or a thrilling promenade on the Great Wall. He might have even downed a soothing bowl of wonton soup while he tried to find a solution to his latest scheduling dilemma.

The obvious solution to any of my travel dilemmas has always been to visit as many great cities as possible. And so in my case, the answer is a no brainer: Beijing or bust!

Beijing's stupendous coming out party, better known as the 2008 Summer Olympics, was only one stunning example of the meteoric development that has taken place in the city. The new China Syndrome is something that the world will continue to experience for years to come. Beijing is growing faster than Pinocchio's nose. If you stand still for more then 20 minutes, there will be a brand new skyscraper hot off the assembly line ready to be filled with venture capitalists and technology giants. The speed with which the city is changing is mind bending. One has only to look at the superb, world class architecture that was created for the Olympics to know how far China has come. The Chinese government has gone to great lengths to make Beijing the poster city for the new China at its

continued on page 176

most fabulous.

But all this building and expanding comes at a high price. You can't breathe (nor could the Olympians, for that matter), with ease. Not only are you surrounded by people smoking, 24/7, the air is often thick with industrial pollution. To make matters even grittier, Beijing is just a hop, skip and a camel ride from the great Gobi Desert, so there are frequent dust storms that whip through the city and deposit a layer of sand on everything. Asthmatics and the allergy prone, beware.

One expat resident of Beijing said that he felt he was living at the beach. There is, however, some hope on Beijing's hazy horizon. The government has begun to take drastic measures such as not permitting heavy trucks to enter the city until nightfall. But for the present, the theme song in Beijing is "Smog Gets in Your Eyes."

As the city morphs into a great metropolis, familiar landmarks are being swallowed whole. Gone are most of the winding, narrow alleys from another century, the "hutongs" and their cozy courtyard houses. The new is squeezing out the old and the charming.

Once I figured it out, I found the restaurant scene in Beijing to be an exciting aspect of the city. Not only did the city successfully cope with feeding the hordes who came for the Olympics, it

Beijing Duck

Photo by Toby Oxborrow

managed its growing pains with seemingly ease, and has become a welcoming culinary capital.

In many ways, the Chinese are valiantly trying to adjust to brand new lives in circumstances still changing from week to week. The question seems to be: Can they mingle the old with the new now that they find themselves between a wok and a hard place?

It's not hard to understand why travelers who visit Beijing believe that since they're in the capital of China, every block will be lined with outstanding Chinese restaurants. But it's sad

that many are sure they will almost certainly be familiar with what's listed on the menu. Think again.

This misconception may be due to years of brainwashing by those Chinese restaurants in the United States that offered or still offer the all-purpose combination plate or the no-surprises-here take-out menu. Far too many tourists came of travel age with glorious visions of chicken chow mien and egg drop soup dancing in their heads.

Most restaurants I visited in Beijing served Pekinese or Mandarin cuisine. Mandarin usually describes recipes that were originated for the imperial court, such as Peking duck and hot and sour soup, while Pekinese is made up of simpler, more casual fare such as dim sum and vegetable dishes.

Generally speaking, restaurant menus in Beijing are not as user friendly as the ones in Hong Kong. A menu in English was once as hard to find as a pastrami sandwich. Today, some top restaurants offer menus with translations while some less-expensive ones show photos of their offerings, although the pictures may be a puzzlement themselves. As tourism marches on, new restaurants are springing up as rapidly as the new construction. Keeping up with the food scene in Beijing has become its own Olympic event.

Newer hotel restaurants, however, tend to be comfortable and familiar. If, however, you desire to explore more interesting choices, it's usually the locals who know about those hidden gems that thrill food-aholics. You are most likely to find them—if you are fluent in Mandarin or are accompanied by someone who is. Be warned that there are parts of this large city where an address is merely a state of mind.

FANGSHAN – #54

After a long, hot day walking the Great Wall, the need for sustenance always trumps the need for shoe repair. My own visit to the Great Wall would have made Humpty Dumpty proud. Unfortunately, I tripped right in front of a group of German tourists who had a really hard time putting me back together again. After such a humiliating experience, I needed more than a double martini and an order of dumplings for dinner. The only way I could make amends for slipping the light fantastic was to make my chopsticks click in double time at Fangshan.

Posh is not a word one often uses when speaking of Beijing restaurants but "Fangshan" which means "imperial," is said to serve dishes that were once prepared for the last emperor of China, Puyi himself. The restaurant was opened in 1925 by cooks who had worked at the imperial court in the early 1900s during Puyi's very short reign. It's really cool to think that some of the selections that appear on Fangshan's menu were at one time dished up in the Forbidden City. The very young emperor seemed to have been partial to meat because Fangshan is a carnivore's delight. It has, at any given time, lamb roast, pork roast, pork chops, lamb chops, deer, turtle and steak

Courtesy of Kinabaloo

on the menu and that doesn't even include the specials of the day.

The lamb shank that I ordered was barbequed and served sizzling right off the spit. It was pink and perfect. Fangshan also offers a 14 course dinner made up of imperial dishes which I thought best, considering my short stay in Beijing, to forego. One of the other selections that I decided to pass on was Camel's Paw. I always thought camels had hooves, but apparently not at Fangshan.

Perhaps the management tends to push the theatrical button a bit too forcefully, since the room is a sea of red and gilt, with vivid murals that cover the ceiling. The serving staff is dressed as if they could perform *Flower Drum Song* at a moment's notice. The outdoor setting for the restaurant is much calmer. Fangshan sits at the edge of a placid lake in a small park. If you're really fortunate, there will be dancers in imperial costume performing on the lawn.

FANGSHAN/ BEIHAI PARK/ EAST GATE/ TEL:
   6401-1889-1879
Expensive

FANGSHAN'S MILIEU

After dinner and all that gilded grandeur, a walk around the lake would make for a tranquil restorative. More of the park can be explored after lunch or early in the evening. Since Fangshan is a bit off the beaten track it would be best to take a cab to and from the restaurant.

XIAN LAO MAN – #55

Unlike Fangshan, Xian Lao is definitely *not* an outpost of the Imperial Palace but, no matter, when you need a dumpling fix think Xian Lao Man. The décor consists of monumentally large glass jars of preserved garlic and ginger. But as Confucius might say these are very good omens.

   The dumplings served at Xian Lao Man are made with amazing speed and dexterity while you watch, and they disappear almost as quickly. The dough is so delicate and silky that if you're not careful you may have consumed a dozen or two before you even know it. As that old saying goes, a dumpling a day keeps the acupuncturist away.

Other delicious things are served at Xian Lao Man but if you ask anyone on the long line that keeps lengthening as you wait, you'll hear pretty much the same thing from most of them. They've come for dumplings! These tiny tender tidbits are made with a variety of stuffings but no matter which you pick you'll find, as I did, that they are all seriously terrific. The more I write about them, the more I find myself thinking that it's time to go back and investigate further.

Xian Lao Man/ 252 Andingmennei Dajie/ Dongcheng District/ Tel: 8610-6404-9644
Inexpensive

 ## XIAN LAO MAN'S MILIEU

Most areas in Beijing are best explored block by block, and the Dongcheng District, where Xian Lao Man is located, is no exception. It's crowded with small temples, shops and food stalls, and they're all open late into the evening. Language here, as in most places in Beijing, will be somewhat of a problem, however pointing always seems to work. And a word about the inscrutable: the golden rule when traveling in Asia is, always have a card from your hotel to give to your cab driver. Otherwise, you may never see your clothes again.

LIQUN – #56

Don't even try to find the actual entrance to this state secret. It's hard enough to find the district and then the name of the road. Once you've

located the road, all you have to do is hail a trishaw (tricycle-style rickshaw) to take you deep into the narrow alley (hutong) where Liqun is, you hope, to be found. Is all this worth it? The answer is, of course, *yes*—that is if you want the best Beijing duck in Beijing.

Liqun may be renowned for its superbly lacquered and aromatic Beijing Duck but

it's certainly not known for its superb ambiance. Just walking through the kitchen, dodging the pyromaniacal flames that lap at you from under the huge woks, adds an exciting note of danger to the whole experience. For me, it was love at first sight. I found that the rough and tumble crowds, the bare tables and brusque service only served to heighten my expectations.

The old timers who grew up in the city when it was called Peking still refer to the duck of

(continued on page 186)

Photo by docsdl

 Cabbage Dumplings/
Meatball Dumplings

For dumpling packets

- *1 cup water*
- *2 cups wheat or rice flour (Beijing cooks prefer wheat-flour but south China cooks insist that their rice-flour dumpling packets are more floaty).*

Cabbage Filling

- *1 small cabbage*
- *Salted water*
- *Sichuan peppercorn or other hot pepper of your choice*
- *½ teaspoon salt*
- *3 tablespoons peanut oil*

Meat Dumpling Filling

- *Ground (finally chopped or minced) meat of your choice*
- *Finely chopped ginger*
- *Finely chopped garlic*
- *Chopped scallions*
- *Chicken broth*
- *Soy sauce*
- *Sesame oil*
- *Cucumber (optional side addition)*

Early Packet Preparation

Put flour in a bowl. Dribble in water while kneading for five to 15 minutes. The more you work the dough, the lighter the dumpling. Cover bowl with damp cloth, and let dough sit for 1 hour for it to soften.

Cabbage Filling Preparation

Peel leaves off cabbage and soak them in a bowl half or more filled with salted water for 1 hour. Pour out and dispose of salted water.

Place warm peanut oil in wok. Add peppercorn, let soak for a minute or two then dispose of pepper.

Place cabbage leaves in wok. Add ½ teaspoon of salt. Cook over fairly-hot heat for a minute but be careful not to sear leaves. Turn off heat. Reserve at room temperature to use as dumpling filler.

Or you can prepare the cabbage just before you finally boil up the filled dumplings and serve it as a hot first dish to stay hunger while your family or guests wait for something more substantial.

Meat Dumpling Filling

A little ground meat goes a long way in making these dumplings, each filled with a marble-size meatball. You can either use ground pork or ground chicken or a combination of both. The important thing here is the ratio of chopped meat to flour,

you'll want about a third of your mixture to be meat. Two-thirds of the mixture will be flour and the following: finely chopped scallion tops, garlic and ginger. Season strongly or lightly, according to taste. Add a few drops of sesame oil to help ingredients cohere.

Use one hand to stir meat mixture clockwise (for good luck) with a pair of wood chopsticks. Then use your fingers to roll your mixed ingredients into tiny meatballs.

Bring chicken broth to boil over high heat. You'll want enough to just or almost cover your meatballs. If you like saltiness, add a teaspoon of soy sauce to the broth and mix it in.

Skin and dice some cucumber, if you like. And reserve to serve with the meat dumplings.

Drop seasoned meatballs into boiling broth. Watch it—as soon as the water has steamed off, your meatballs are done.

Finishing the dumplings

For each set of 15 dumplings, you'll need water to fill your wok half way or more, plus ½ cup to 1½ cups cold (room-temperature) water to set aside.

Lightly flour a wood tabletop or board. (Use the same flour you used in making the dumpling dough.) Wake your resting dough from its long wait and hand roll into a long, sausage shape. Sprinkle more flour on your board as needed to prevent sticking. Pinch off small pieces of your dough sausage.

Use the palm of your hand to roll each snippet into a round shape. Use a small (two to three inch in diameter) rolling pin or wood cylinder to roll out each small dough circle into a two or three inch disc.

Use chopsticks (or a small spoon, if you must) to pick up cabbage or meat filling and drop filling into the center of a dough disc. Fold up dumpling and pinch it closed, working from the center outward. You'll want to prepare for cooking at least 15 dumplings at a time. But you can fold up more envelopes at this time, too.

Boil water in wok. Add 15 dumplings. This will cool the water some. Wait for the water to boil up again. When it's again going full throttle, add ½ cup of colder water. Repeat two more times. After the third dash of cold or room-temp water, your dumplings should be floating on top of your wok, signifying that they are done. Your total cooking time for 15 dumplings should take no longer than seven or eight minutes.

Serving

Some people offer the cabbage mixture as a warm separate dish to eat while the dumplings boil. Others use it as a dumpling filling.

Chopped raw cucumber makes a cool complement to the meat dumplings.

Sheng Xueni suggests for either dumpling, or both, a dipping sauce made of equal parts soy sauce and rice vinegar, with chili added (or not) to taste. A good cook boils only 15 dumplings at a time, so they're fresh and hot.

Recipes courtesy of Sheng Xueni, Beijing hutong cook

MAKES 24 TO 30 SMALL DUMPLINGS

their dreams as "Peking Duck." But no matter what it's called, it is to Beijing what pastrami is to New York or barbequed brisket is to Dallas. The question is, what becomes a Peking legend most? The menu at Liqun is devoted to answering that very question. For a really ducky experience, the little rascals are served in the classic manner with steamed pancakes. If you prefer, they can be roasted, sautéed, glazed or barbequed. And by an obvious bit of de-duck-tion, even duck tongues (don't ask) are available here, as a side dish.

LIQUN /11 BEIXANGFENG ALLEY /ZHENGYI ROAD / CHONGWEN DISTRICT/ TEL: 86-10-6705-5578
UNLIKE OTHER BEIJING RESTAURANTS, YOU MUST RESERVE AT LEAST 7 DAYS IN ADVANCE.
Moderate

🎈 LIQUN'S MILIEU

Make your way out of the winding alley that houses Liqun and try to catch a cab. Never miss an opportunity to hail one of Beijing's relatively inexpensive taxis since the city is enormous and tends to be confusing. However, that shouldn't inhibit your après-duck exploration. I'm not an advocate of too much pre-programming but perhaps you can make a plan before your visit to Liqun and rely on your cab driver to take you over to one of the main streets so that you can stroll in a whole new area.

Beijing/
Front Burner

If you've never visited the original Raffles Hotel in Singapore, you can still win a prize by dropping into its new Beijing outpost. I'm told that its Afternoon Tea Buffet served daily in its Jaan Restaurant is a sumptuous spread overflowing with delights, both Asian and British.

JAAN, RAFFLES HOTEL/ 33 EAST CHANG AN AVENUE/ TEL: 6526-3388-4186

Shanghai

"By midday the Tankadere was only about 45 miles from Shanghai. It had only six hours left to reach the port."

—Jules Verne

So near and yet so far. Phileas thought he had finally overcome his missed connection from Hong Kong by hiring a boat to get him to Shanghai. The good news was that from there he could continue on and, in the nick of time, catch the steamer to San Francisco. The bad news was that just to keep the pot boiling, Verne never let Phileas actually get to Shanghai. That most definitely, was bad news.

The Shanghai of Phileas' day was a great deal more unsavory than it is today. Shanghai Lil, one of the town's more notorious ladies of the evening at the turn of the 19th century, is long gone with the intrigue and other questionable pleasures that Shanghai was once famous for. In the 1900s, sailors were routinely drugged and kidnapped from Shanghai's seedy waterfront bars and sold to unscrupulous sea captains. When the seamen woke up they were on their way to nowhere but trouble. Thus the word "shanghaied" became part

of the English vocabulary. Today, the luxury cruise ships that dock in Shanghai will only kidnap you if you bring them a boatload of money.

The British as well as the deposed last emperor of China used Shanghai as their personal playground. A whiff of seduction coupled with the scent of danger made it the perfect place to set a novel or have an affair. In the 1920s, Noel Coward wrote *Private Lives* while living in Shanghai and dancing the nights away in its posh clubs. In those days, everyone associated Shanghai with both lavish excess and drop-dead glamour. The good times came to a screeching halt when Shanghai suffered through the brutality of the Japanese invasion, and then its own countrymen's rage during the '60s Cultural Revolution. One can only think that its tempestuous past has helped to make the Shanghai of today one of the more intriguing major cities of the world.

In terms of temperament, Shanghai could

not be more dissimilar to Beijing. Unlike its far more conservative sister, Shanghai vibrates with sophistication and cosmopolitan style. Its shops and hotels resemble those of Paris more than those of China's capital, and the name of its game is money and power. Chinese government leaders know that if they play their mahjong right they can make Shanghai a 21st century Hong Kong but more controllable. The new Shanghai, unlike the still resistant Hong Kong, is truly "People's Republic."

The faded, glories of Shanghai's colonial past include dozens of Victorian mansions and stunning Art Deco villas, as well as a taste for afternoon tea more suited to Chelsea than China. Even today, a stroll down the Bund, the grand promenade on the Huangpu River that houses Shanghai's most important European banks, is a somewhat bittersweet reminder of its former worldly ties.

When I last visited Shanghai, just a few years ago, it was clear that a page had finally been turned. The vibrant Shanghai with its insatiable growth and cutting edge architecture (more than 2000 new skyscrapers), its remaining Art Deco embellishments and its rich, fashionable population is finally becoming what it was always meant to be: one of the great cities of the world. Its huge 2010-2011 fair, with extravagont pavillions raised by countries from all over the globe, accented this.

The Oriental Pearl TV Tower dominates part of Shanghai's skyline. China ~189~

The food scene in Shanghai tends to honor the city's new character which translates into freshness, fragrance and presentation. The most famous of Shanghai's specialties is "drunken chicken" and although the birds don't actually attend AA meetings, they are steeped in enough wine to feel no pain. Most of the other menu headliners depend on fresh-caught hairy crab and almost every other conceivable kind of shellfish.

The dining establishments around town not only represent all corners of China; new restaurants are opening daily that showcase chefs from around the world. They've come to seek their fortune cookies as well as bedazzle the locals with an array of non-Sino presentations. A perfect case in point is Jean-Georges Vongerichten, that master of "Nouvelle Cuisine."

JEAN GEORGES SHANGHAI – #57

Even though Jean Georges is almost a household name among the truly well fed in America, when I visit a culinary venue as exciting as China I usually can't bring myself to focus on a restaurant that is not of the country. It has always seemed to me a colossal waste to eat continental food when I'm not on the continent in question. Of course there will always be exceptions but in general, if I'm in China, why order Veal Prince Orloff?

Now back to Jean Georges and his wonderful venture in Shanghai. I dropped in because the press about it was so intriguing and I thought if I just went for tea in the afternoon, I could still maintain my local-food-only discipline. While I was there I must confess that I couldn't resist

having more than one of his maniacally sinful desserts. Everything chocolate, his variations on a chocolate theme were seriously impressive not to mention seriously caloric. They included a white chocolate parfait studded with raisins and lime, a velvety chocolate caramel mousse showered in a fine grind of Sichuan pepper and, to top it all off, a chocolate cookie with beet and raspberry jam—a chocoholic's fantasy come true. Its only competition might have been the posh surroundings I was devouring all this in, as well as the view, overlooking the tranquil Huangpu River.

Jean Georges is the perfect place to relax and drink in the serene atmosphere as well as a cup of musky, deep green tea.

As for the rest of the menu, the *foie gras* served with star anise flowers and the steamed snapper with basil puree—I might some day allow myself the privilege of making their acquaintance.

But not before I've made a couple of more appearances in more of the great, more typically Shanghainese temples of gastronomy. Then and only then will I throw my chopsticks to the wind.

JEAN-GEORGE/ 3 ZHONGSHAN EAST ROAD
(FOURTH FLOOR)/ TEL: 86-21-6321-7733
Expensive

JEAN GEORGES' MILIEU

Walk along the Huangpu River and explore the Bund, the dazzling new/old financial district of Shanghai. Amid the latest architectural amazements there are the beautiful Art Deco treasures that once housed some of Europe's greatest banks. Try to stop at Sassoon House, built by Victor Sassoon, in the '20s. At the time, he was the most famous of Shanghai's many banking tycoons. If Lalique glass makes you swoon, it did the same for Sir Victor, and the lobby of the building is filled with some of the famous glassmaker's most beautiful designs.

LU BO LANG – #58

We try, sometimes without success, to avoid stuffed shirts but how about stuffed buns? Shanghai takes its stuffed buns very seriously, and so do I. The buns at Lu Bo Lang are not so much stuffed as crammed with all manner of scrumptious things: steamed crab, sautéed prawns, oysters, duck, succulent barbequed pork. The buns themselves are meltingly moist and light enough to almost levitate off your plate (I said almost).

Lu Bo Lang echoes the feeling of old Shanghai, and is filled with regulars who seem to be part of another age. It's the perfect place to escape from

Photo by Jill Shih

the cosmopolitan throngs and step into the past. It's also the perfect place to polish off a plate of Lu Bo's mouth watering buns. The rest of the menu is pure Shanghainese, including its own outstanding version of Drunken Chicken.

Lu Bo Lang/ 115 Yuyuan Road / Huangpu/ no phone

Inexpensive

LU BO LANG'S MILIEU

If you're feeling adventuress you might just want to explore some of the small Buddhist temples to be found all around Lu Bo Lang. I couldn't help stopping to light a joss stick or two. I felt it was the least I could do after having all those ethereal buns.

CRYSTAL JADE – #59

Dim sum junkies, and I count myself as one of the more addicted, need to feed our craving no matter where we go. But when we get to China the need becomes almost insatiable. After all, it's

the mother ship for dumpling lovers the world over. In Shanghai, the place for the dim sum dependent would be Crystal Jade.

Almost too handsome to be a place that is focused mainly on little doughy morsels that drip, not only onto the table but also down the front of my

new silk jacket, Crystal Jade is Dumpling Central in Shanghai. It's the kind of place where one can polish off a plateful of fried pork dumplings with spicy pickled radish in short order. Or if dumplings are not on your personal agenda (perish the thought) then how about trying a crisp fried wonton (really a dumpling in disguise) served with a fiery-hot chili sauce?

Even though the Crystal Jade I chose (one in a familiar chain around town) lives on the second floor of a rather mundane shopping mall, the restaurant itself is a dramatic, glassed-in, two story space covered with mirrors that reflect not only the crowds but also the towers of small

Courtesy of Crystal Jade Group

wicker steamers that decorate each table. Don't expect the usual rolling carts and roaming servers here. Not only is everything made to order but made as soon *as* ordered. No waiting until Chinese New Year, and then delivered cold to your table.

Crystal Jade is not only known for its dim sum, but also for its homemade pulled noodles topped with meat sauce, and its Shanghai soup dumplings, those small pillows with a surprise center filled with scalding broth. The best way to eat them without having to make a trip to the Mayo Clinic is to carefully bite an opening in the dough with your teeth. Then, after a moment or two as the broth cools, suck it out ever so gently, and savor it for a moment before wolfing down the rest of the dumpling. Not worth the effort you say? I guess you've never had a genuine Shanghai soup dumpling!

CRYSTAL JADE/ SOUTH BLOCK/ XINTIANDI/ HOUSE 6-7, LANE 123/ TEL: 8621-6385-8752
Moderate

 CRYSTAL JADE'S MILIEU

The shopping mall that houses this restaurant is an opportunity to test your ability to survive sensory overload. Exploring it will give you and your credit cards quite a workout.

BAO LUO – #60

Every one has certainly heard the phrase "cheap Chinese" but Bao Luo gives new meaning to that phrase while serving up some of the best food in Shanghai.

To mark its entrance, Bao Luo has nothing but a tiny sign done in red neon—just to let you know that you've arrived. It doesn't even have its whole name on the outside, just BL. Now that's what I call confidence. And it's well deserved, judging by the crowds who vie for one of its coveted tables.

Holding almost 300 ravenous patrons at any given time, Bao Luo is the kind of place where friends meet and then hang out for hours. The Seinfeld gang would have been right at home here. Maybe that's why it's so hard to get a table.

You could say that Bao Luo serves up Shanghai soul food. Typical are the crab and pork meatballs. Who knows how many plates of those luscious, mini-spheres Bao serves in a day? You can bet that

BAO LUO'S MILIEU

Fumin Lu is in an area that is filled with bookstores. Don't be deterred because most of the books are in Chinese. Shanghai has such an international profile, there may be sections devoted to Chinese novels that have been translated into English, or perhaps you'll find book illustrations that are more than worthy of framing. How can you possibly resist such a golden literary opportunity? The street also hosts a clutch of small calligraphy shops, and dealers who stock art supplies. You will be in a neighborhood of infinite gift possibilities.

it's enough to keep a small army sated. It's clear that Bao Luo is the kind of place that feeds the spirit as well as the body.

BAO LUO/2721 FUMIN LU/ TEL: 8621-6279-2827

Shanghai/
Front Burner

MR. AND MRS. BUND

If you're maxed out on Shanghainese specialties, why not try French chef Paul Pairet's Asian spin on the usual French suspects? Pairet's recent Gallic addition to the Shanghai restaurant scene became an instant haunt for the town's boldfaced names.

The reports are that Mr. and Mrs. Bund remains a cool place to be seen.

6/F BUND 1818 ZHONGSHAN DONG YI LU/ THE BUND/ TEL: 6323-9898

CRYSTAL JADE GOLDEN PALACE

If one Crystal Jade in Shanghai is terrific (as I indicated in my Shanghai restaurant selections) then two would have to be even more terrific. At a newer Crystal Jade Golden Palace, the management has given the menu a healthier spin and is actually offering less salt, oil and sugar to lighten the profile of some of their presentations.

Not only that but they've added an extensive wine cellar, which is unusual for a Chinese restaurant. Can sommeliers be far behind?

CRYSTAL JADE GOLDEN PALACE/ 290 ORCHARD ROAD/ TEL: 6734-6866

San Francisco

"The ground floor of the hotel was occupied by a large bar, a sort of restaurant freely open to all passers-by. Who might partake of dried beef, oyster soup, biscuits, and cheese without taking out their purses. Payment was only for the ale, porter or sherry which was drunk. This seemed very American to Passepartout."

—Jules Verne

STEAMING ACROSS THE PACIFIC, on the General Grant, with not a nanosecond to spare, Phileas was eager to get to San Francisco. He knew that if all went well from this point on he was sure to arrive back in London, triumphantly, on the 80th day. The General Grant obliged by taking only 11 days to accomplish the voyage to San Francisco, which at the time was considered lightning speed.

While Passepartout was evidently impressed with the generous food and drink he found in San Francisco, it was the spirited temperament of the city that caught the attention of his boss during his one-day stopover.

continued on page 198

Right: Had Phileas Fogg's ship been greeted by the Golden Gate, he, too, might have lost his heart to San Francisco. But although he feared running late, he was a half century too early for the bridge.

In the years that followed the Gold Rush the city could erupt at a moment's notice during a contentious political rally. When Phileas, through no fault of his own, suddenly found himself in the middle of just such a riot, he found it necessary to fend off a member of the unruly mob. In his utter disdain for such barbarous behavior his only comment to his attacker was, "Yankee!"

My introduction to San Francisco lacked the violent drama of Fogg's. For me it was love at first sight. And to this date, the image of the Golden Gate Bridge hanging over the bay makes my eyes mist over. My friends like to call me the "Will Rogers of travel" since I've never met a destination I didn't like, and I suppose they're right. But my fascination with San Francisco is that it makes you work really hard to understand it. It can't be characterized by its population or its ravishing location. It's a city that thrives on exciting new ideas, controversial attitudes and stubborn convictions. San Francisco reminds me of an oyster with a grain of sand slowly driving it crazy. Any irritant that affects this city is rolled around, roiled and reshaped until it ultimately becomes a brand new pearl in its progressive society.

Its political awareness might derive from the fact that the city was built on the dreams of an army of prospectors who came to mine the earth for riches. That dream continued to drive San

Francisco's urban psyche, long after the Gold Rush was a glittering memory.

Leaving one's heart in San Francisco is not uncommon. Just ask Tony Bennett. The city is a fog-shrouded Brigadoon that rises out of the haze not every hundred years but each day, to enchant residents and visitors alike. Despite the fact that the earth has, on occasion, been known to tremble beneath one's feet, and the weather has no relationship to the calendar, no one seems to mind. An anonymous wag once said, "The coldest winter I ever spent was the summer I visited San Francisco."

Today, the rush in San Francisco is not for gold but to the trendiest restaurant, the yet undiscovered wine shop, the coffee house with the most brilliant brew or that ever so charming little boutique hotel. People are still mining but for a whole new kind of treasure.

Food in San Francisco is more of a spiritual experience than a culinary one. People count restaurants as places of worship, second only to the ones with stained glass windows. Instead of men of the cloth they look to men of the kitchens for guidance. San Franciscans are gastro-intellectuals; they eat to think, not to live. For those lucky enough to reside here, the appreciation of the restaurant scene is fed by an embarrassment of riches. Not surprisingly, San

Franciscans are very much like the French in feeling that no matter where they travel nothing quite compares with the everyday excellence they already enjoy.

All of this reverence for restaurants of all shapes and sizes and cuisines may be traced back to the city's Gold Rush days. The men that poured into San Francisco, armed with picks, shovels and pans, forgot to bring their pots. More important, they forgot to bring their wives or significant others. It became painfully clear to these hungry honeys that there was little possibility of a home-cooked meal. The only thing to look forward to was a dinner served communally at their boarding houses. Getting together at meal time was a chance to feel a bit less lonely and, in time, eating out became a way of life in San Francisco.

Of course, the miners were not the only ones who came to San Francisco to seek their fortunes.

Immigrants arrived from all over the world. Instead of looking for gold in the mines, they looked for gold in the pockets of those lucky enough to strike it rich. They were the ones who set up the restaurants and became the cooks who would eventually bring fine dining to a city that had never even heard of table manners.

The San Francisco of today overflows with the riches of California's culinary treasure chest. Just a short drive from the city, there are countless small boutique farms as well as independent cheese makers committed to supplying the best of the best to the city's super-particular chefs. And then, of course, there is San Francisco's bottomless wine glass, courtesy of some of the most respected yet nearby vineyards in the world. You could say, without fear of exaggeration, San Francisco's cup overflows.

TADICH GRILL – #61

The restaurant scene in San Francisco is an ever changing canvas. Even so, there are still more than a few golden oldies in the city's gastronomic landscape. One very good choice is Tadich Grill.

You have to feel a bit in awe of anything that's over 150 years old, except for me, of course.

But the Tadich Grill, venerable though it may be, is just-plain-folks to the folks who've been coming here most of their lives. And this includes the bankers and CEOs who love to hang out. Perhaps they're influenced by the Tadich's humble beginning.

It started as a hastily constructed coffee stand, set up to serve the men who were rushing to the Gold Rush. They would stop, grab a cup o' joe and then head for San Francisco's 18 carat hills. When Tadich finally grew up to become a real restaurant, no expense was spared. It was done in solid mahogany paneling with a long bar to match. That's the very bar you see as you enter. When I first stepped through the door there was never any doubt that I was in one of the city's landmarks, even though Tadich wears its fame with a great deal of modesty.

Be prepared for a ginormous menu. No small card filled with the chef's whims of the day. It goes on and on from steak to chops to stews to chowders to burgers to endless salad choices and, of course, the umpteen daily specials. However, if you believe the words of many happy mouths, Tadich means only one thing: fish. The sautéed sand dabs and grilled swordfish done over mesquite are among the best in the city. And everything tastes even better because it's served with the yeasty sourdough bread San Francisco is famous for. Most of the locals don't even bother to pick up the menu. They just look at their waiter and ask, in an expectant voice, "What's in today?" If only all life was as simple as it is at the Tadich Grill.

TADICH GRILL/ 240 CALIFORNIA STREET/ TEL: 415-391-1849
Moderate

TADICH GRILL'S MILIEU

California Street is steep enough to roll down or climb up—your choice may depend on the shape you're in. Having just consumed a gargantuan meal at Tadich, the best option might be the former. Once you've negotiated the geography, you can make your way over to Montgomery Street and one of the city's signature buildings: the Transamerica. Its distinctive four-sided pyramid design makes this building the most recognizable symbol in San Francisco's skyline.

BOULEVARD – #62

Think back to the San Francisco of the 1890s and 1900s: music halls, bawdy babes, instant millionaires and the rough-and-tumble Barbary Coast. These colorful images conjure up a city devoted to the joys of excess. If I were asked to name the one restaurant in San Francisco that would make me think of those excessively golden days, it would have to be Boulevard.

Housed in the Audiffred Building, at the foot of Mission Street, Boulevard echoes the Belle Époque of Paris in all of its lavish romanticism. The Audiffred Building itself was built in 1889. It was one of the few that survived the earthquake of 1906, and just barely at that. The firemen were about to dynamite the building to stop the fire line from spreading but, in the nick of time, the wind changed and the building was saved. The Audiffred today serves to give Boulevard a landmark setting.

Dinner at Boulevard is, for many reasons, a grand occasion. One of the more important of these is its star-studded chef, Nancy Oakes. Ever since she opened its doors in 1993, Boulevard has attracted the *haute* polloi of the city. Oakes' dazzling menu is sophisticated and creative. Her accent is unabashedly American but there's a whiff of France that only adds to the individuality of

BOULEVARD'S MILIEU

The Embarcadero area along San Francisco Bay is one of the loveliest walks in the city. It may be a bit longer than most of the suggested milieu walks but it passes some really great sights. One of them is the historic Ferry Building, opened in 1898 to serve the ferry boats that brought passengers from the East Bay. The Ferry Building has been converted into a farmers market as well as a place for purchase of gourmet prepared foods and informal fine dining. If you continue north and than veer west along the Embarcadero, you'll eventually reach Ghirardelli Square for some souvenir shopping and some great views, not to mention a chocolate bar or two. There's also a wonderful aquarium near the square, in case you didn't order fish for dinner.

her food. And happily, she relies on the seasons to inform her menu. One of the things I have never failed to order at Boulevard is the pan seared foie gras wearing just a thin drizzle of tart rhubarb syrup. Unfortunately, this will soon be a delicious memory, as the preparation of foie gras has been banned in California, as of 2012. Boulevard, for the moment, is cooking in great style.

The dramatic views of the Bay Bridge from the windows confirm the fact that Boulevard is definitely not in Paris. But with its Art Nouveau accents, the lush floral arrangements and the elegant vaulted ceilings, the sensibilities of the City of Light are very much a part of the scene. One of the true pleasures in life is having superb food in beautiful surroundings (only after achieving world peace, a stable economy and saving the planet, that is), and Boulevard definitely fits that bill.

BOULEVARD/ 1, MISSION STREET,
    EMBARCADERO/ TEL: 415-543-6084
Very Expensive

SWAN OYSTER DEPOT – #63

Yet another landmark in San Francisco, this time an oyster house that shucked its very first shell in 1912.

In San Francisco, the resident experts all agree that the Swan Oyster Depot is the pearl of the seafood set. You have to think breakfast or lunch at Swan's because dinner is not on the menu. And just to prepare you, there are no tables, chairs or other signs of gentility. When I stop by, as I do whenever I'm in town, I climb up on a stool at the long marble counter and name the number of those bi-valve beauties that my heart desires . . . six, twelve, a bushel? Anything goes at this

Courtesy of Swan Oyster Depot

friendly outpost for crustacean appreciation. While you're downing your sparklingly fresh, briny delights, people are choosing from the fresh fish in the market part of the diner. The atmosphere is pure San Francisco.

If oysters "R" never in season for you, Swan's, which is still family owned, always has something fishy going on. There is an extensive menu covering all the other categories of edible ocean life. The cold crab salad and the homemade chowders may not be on the half shell but they're terrific, too.

SWAN OYSTER DEPOT/ 1517 POLK STREET/ TEL: 415-673-1101/BREAKFAST AND LUNCH ONLY *Moderate*

SWAN OYSTER DEPOT'S MILIEU

When you hear the name Nob Hill, I'll bet you think of wealth and power. Well, you'd be right on the money. After the Gold Rush days, Nob Hill became home to the city's railroad barons as well as the rest of the super rich. In fact, it used to be called "Snob Hill." Whatever, it was swank with a capital dollar sign. Most of the grand mansions were destroyed in the 1906 earthquake and never rebuilt. There are one or two left but the area has since been filled by five star hotels, restaurants and shops. The Fairmont Hotel, which sits on the site of one of those great homes, is a capital choice in which to have a drink.

GARY DANKO – #64

Think celebrity chef, and in San Francisco Gary Danko immediately springs to mind. No matter how many flashes in the pan come and go, Danko remains at the top of San Francisco's food chain. His books and local TV appearances have made him a cottage industry in the city. He has also managed to snag the coveted Five Diamond Award for excellence from the Mobil Travel Guide, and that's not chopped liver.

Everyone seems to be dressed in Armani at Danko, not only the diners but even the wait staff. Danko is super-chef territory and has all the right accessories to prove it. The cuisine is identified on the menu as New American, one of those vague

descriptions that seems to imply that there is an Old American. We all know by now what they're really trying to say is lighter, natural ingredients, healthy and artfully presented. It's Gary Danko's flawless execution of exceptional ingredients that sets his food apart. He seems committed to not only using locally grown, seasonal ingredients but to pairing them with exotic elements from Asia and beyond. His pan-seared shellfish with Thai curry makes for a dynamite combination. West meets East and they both appear to enjoy the confrontation.

The restaurant is as perfect as its owner-chef. The carefully designed, minimalist décor is lean and smart with tables set far enough apart for diners to have a quiet disagreement without fear of raising eyebrows. Tall shutters and wood paneling soften the super-modern edges.

Danko is dear to my heart, aside from the chef's brilliance because it has one of the best cheese services around. No matter how tempting the menu and how many things I yearn to order, I manage to think ahead to the pleasures of the

GARY DANKO'S MILIEU

A half-hour stroll on North Point Street can lead you down to Fisherman's Wharf which is near Pier 39. The Wharf is home to several seafood restaurants and carts, more interesting to look at than to eat at. As a bonus, the wharf has a booth where you can book a trip out to Alcatraz—of your own free will. In the old days it was ever so much easier to get to Alcatraz than to get back. Pier 39 is a huge complex filled with shops and souvenirs that's always crowded with tourists.

cheese cart, which appears pre-dessert. Or in my case, instead. The sommelier always seems to find just the right port to finish off the stilton and pours it with great panache.

GARY DANKO/ 800 NORTH POINT STREET/ TEL: 415-749-2060
Very Expensive

THE FOG CITY DINER – #65

Everybody loves a diner; it's an American symbol of down-to-earth values and casual camaraderie, not to mention the call of the open road. It's our answer to the French bistro and the Italian coffee house. And the fact that it's shiny and covered with chrome doesn't hurt, either. The mystique of the diner lives on as nostalgia is sprinkled over everything like confectioners sugar.

Fog City Diner has almost nothing to do with those tacky, worn out icons that are found in many small towns in America. And it has nothing to do with those supersonic, tricked out faux railroad cars that seem to be popping up in every strip mall or shopping center, nationwide. Though the Fog City Diner wears its metallic façade with pride, its interior is surprisingly urbane and sophisticated. At first I was a bit disappointed by the lack of diner kitsch but to make up for it Fog City has a raw bar, a very cool clientele and an excellent wine list.

The food at Fog City is not confined to old diner standards such as french fries drowned in orange-color cheese sauce (one of my favorites) or greasy burgers topped with greasier fried onions (another of my top ten). Even though burgers and fries and actual milkshakes are available, so are hard liquor and very grown up grills and chops, cioppino (fish stew) and a really spiffy version of mac and cheese made with imported gouda.

Even though the food is not quite up to the lofty standards of the best-of-the-west it's still a fun place for lunch.

THE FOG CITY DINER/ 1300 BATTERY STREET/ TEL:415- 982-2000
Moderate

 THE FOG CITY DINER'S MILIEU

Battery Street leads down to the Embarcadero. During World War II the Embarcadero was a military instillation and the thousands of troops who left for the Pacific embarked from there. Aside from its historic significance, it's a great place if the weather cooperates to watch the fog from the bay slip in to shroud the city. Romance and mystery all rolled into one.

ZUNI CAFÉ – #66

You'd think that Zuni had been in business long enough to have shed its mega-trendy image and calmed itself down. Maybe the bloom is still on this San Francisco hotspot because of its chef Judy Rodgers and her gifted coupling of the Southwest and the Mediterranean. Whatever the reason, Zuni is a hangout for all age groups, which is a rarity. Rodgers' devoted fans love her menu because there's bound to be someone's very favorite thing in the whole world on it. Pasta comes with apple smoked bacon, a thick glazed pork chop nestles next to mashed sweet potatoes

and Rodger's near perfect Caesar salad is always on the menu. Yet another option in her catalogue of winners is a buttery roast chicken served with a Tuscan bread salad that could bring tears to your eyes. Zuni's separate oyster menu has at least 12 varieties at any given time. All of this adds up to one of the most talked about and most enjoyed restaurants in the city.

ZUNI CAFÉ/ 1658 MARKET STREET/ TEL: 415- 552-2522
Moderate

San Francisco/
Front Burner

CHOW

Right at the entrance to the Castro District, Chow is a perfect example of San Francisco's changing scene. The Castro District was once the political cutting edge of the city. Today, it's more like Yuppie Heaven, and its new restaurants reflect the change. One of the best is Chow, looking more like it should have a posh North Beach address; it's a favorite for the 30-something's dating game. You can go for dinner or just sit at the bar with an imported brew and a sandwich. Either way, you'll enjoy the scene.

Chow/ 215 Church Street/
   Tel: 415-552-2469

Chicago

> "Chicago, already risen from its ruins [of the great fire of 1871], and more proudly seated than ever on the borders of its beautiful Lake Michigan."
>
> —Jules Verne

Alas, poor Phileas! His train had been attacked by Indians on the warpath as it was speeding toward Chicago. Not to mention that in those days scalpers were known for giving rather painful haircuts, not tickets to the Super Bowl. What's the central character in a famous adventure novel to do? It was clear that Fogg had a lot more on his mind than the beauty of Lake Michigan.

I must admit that I don't remember anything like that ever happening to me on my way to Chicago but then I was able to wait for a much more accommodating century. Phileas, of course, had his hot date back in 1872. Once Fogg's train arrived in Chicago, he did nothing more than change to another train.

The word "authentic" is used today to describe everything from politicians to popes. Authenticity seems to be the quality of the moment as people search for the genuine article, not just a weak

imitation. Look no further because Chicago is a city that has dedicated itself to being not the first, but the Second City of the United States. What could be more authentic than *not* trying to be number one? You have to love Chicagoans for that.

Even before Mrs. O'Leary and her klutzy cow managed to burn down the city, Chicago was content to accept the fact that it was never going to be New York. Its citizens came to the decision that it was much more important for Chicago to be Chicago. Then or later on, Chicago citizens could have looked for some snazzy signature name, a la "the Big Apple," say, "the Big Pizza." But blowing its horn really isn't Chicago's style. By remaining "the Windy City," Chicago's confidence in its easygoing, good-natured approach is impressive.

Chicago's North Michigan Avenue is regarded

as one of the major boulevards in the country but as you stroll or window shop along the "Magnificent Mile" you never get the feeling that people are pushing or rushing. Not even at rush hour. Not even right before Christmas. They just relax into whatever the situation requires and then go with the flow.

Chicago, perhaps as much as New York, is a city where it pays to look up as you walk its streets. Its architectural diversity and skyline are arresting. Through the years, the city has accumulated a portfolio of exciting buildings built by renowned architects. It has been a creative incubator for names like Frank Lloyd Wright, Mies Van der Rohe and Helmut Jahn. Chicago has often been called the world capital of architecture.

Architecture isn't the only creative force in the city. There are magnificent sculptures by Picasso, Miro, Chagall and Dubuffet as well as newer, riskier names that push younger artistic envelopes.

Chicago has plenty of theatrical and comedic talents, who, having showcased their work at the iconic Second City Theater, have gone on to be national scene stealers. Second City alumni help populate *Saturday Night Live* as well as the Broadway stage. Take David Mamet, for instance. Chicago has also given Winfreyism to the world. Oprah has become Chicago's most recognizable resident and her Harpo Studios is as much of a landmark as the Willis Tower (formerly, the Sears Tower).

The Chicago food scene is either big and glitzy or mom and pop comfy. Several multiethnic storefront eateries have reached the heights of excellence.

As for street food, the sausage on a bun, be it a common frank, a Polish kielbasa or even a German *brat* is one of the city's *wurst* addictions. Chicagoans are more than entitled to bust their buttons over their sausage-mania. After all, they actually invented the frankfurter. Honestly! To be absolutely frank—and despite what many New Yorkers think—the hotdog was first cooked up in Chicago in the 1890s. And no one in Chi Town would ever think of putting mustard on it, just onions, chili sauce and relish. Most important of all, the dog must recline seductively on a poppy seed bun.

Now, about deep dish pizza—that came much later, in the 1930s. It was invented by the Chicago chef who eventually opened the first Pizzeria Uno (now Uno Chicago Grill). His thought was that if he spread the dough on the bottom of a deep pan he could add much more cheese and sauce to the crust. That's American knowhow for you. The entire city of Naples experienced a collective shudder but everyone in Chicago thought that its

numero uno had a real winner.

To return to the big and glitzy: Most people who are familiar with the food scene in Chicago know that Charlie Trotter is the commander in chief. Charlie is a five-time James Beard award winner and a constant inspiration for most of the other chefs in town. Charlie has become a Chicago hero.

CHARLIE TROTTER'S – #67

For over two decades, Charlie Trotter's has been the place to expect the best of everything. His menu is an extension of his art and no one disputes that Charlie is a superb culinary artist. The restaurant echoes the elegance of the menu: clean lines, svelte décor, a minimum of noise and nothing to upstage the extraordinary food. Service, as you would expect, is impeccable, and the prices, as you would also expect, are super-expensive. To quote *Chicago Magazine*, "This is a restaurant like Cape Canaveral is an airport."

The menu at Trotter's is made up of a conservative number of selections, unlike many of Charlie's colleagues who offer page upon page of possibilities. Charlie's menu philosophy has always been more is definitely a great deal less. He is almost obsessively focused on taste, texture and presentation. His keen culinary intellect has led him to the distinctive combining of ingredients that are guaranteed to expand your gastronomic scrapbook. Asparagus soup topped with a delicate gauze of spun honey. Short ribs braised for a breathtaking 48 hours and then, as they fall from the bone, partnered with porcini mushrooms and fermented garlic. Cold poached cod cheek served with an heirloom tomato and Thai basil. Who even knew that a cod had cheeks?

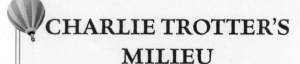

CHARLIE TROTTER'S MILIEU

The best thing about the West Armitage area is that it's loaded with trendy shops to enjoy--- that is, if you still have a bank balance after leaving the restaurant. As you walk over to Milwaukee Avenue, to the north of Armitage, you will be on a street that theoretically will lead you right to the city of Milwaukee. Now that might be a little far for an after dinner stroll but it's so much fun to think about. Milwaukee Avenue follows an old Indian trail.

Charlie chooses to offer three distinct menus: the Grand Menu that has a variety of seasonal dishes, the Vegetarian Menu, which gives new meaning to eating your greens and the Kitchen Menu, which is served to those who manage to reserve the very exclusive chef's table in the kitchen.

Charlie Trotter's mission in life is to challenge the palate and expand the senses. A rousing three cheers, as far as I'm concerned. But to be painfully honest, it doesn't always work. A dessert of Okinawan sweet potato afloat in a pool of stout and covered with marshmallows sounded more like a Wes Craven film than the end of a perfect meal. However, the chocolate custard with kaffir lime more than made up for it.

A visit to Charlie's kitchen (if you ask, you may be able to tour it after dinner) topped off my singular Trotter experience. As impressive as dinner at Charlie Trotter's is, I left feeling that I had been part of something exciting and exhausting at the same time.

CHARLIE TROTTER'S/ 816 WEST ARMITAGE
    AVE./ TEL: 773-248-6228
TWO SEATINGS, 6-6:30, 9-9:30
Painfully Expensive

BILLY GOAT TAVERN – #68

What restaurant inspired John Belushi to shout out, "cheezzssbourrrger, cheezzbourrger, cheezzbourrrger, petsi, petsi, petsi," on Saturday Night Live? You guessed it, the Billy Goat Tavern.

Belushi must have eaten an awful lot of burgers at the Billy Goat to have come up with the sketch that made him famous. Not to mention raising the short-order cook to superstar status on TV, and making Billy Goat Tavern into a Chicago institution. The hilarious Belushi connection came long after the Billy Goat opened in 1934. The story goes that a tavern called the Lincoln was bought for the princely sum of $205. One day a very inquisitive goat fell off a farm truck on the way to market, and wandered into the tavern.

Courtesy of Billy Goat Tavern

The goat was instantly adopted, and from that day on the place was known as the Billy Goat Tavern. It became so popular that the owner decided to go the extra mile and name himself Billy Goat. He even grew a goatee. The motto of the tavern is "Butt in anytime" and that's exactly what I do when I get to Chicago. For me, Billy Goat is a really great joint and the "cheezzbourrrrgers" are actually pretty good.

To ease the mind of any goat-a-phobes, there are no goat delicacies on the menu, not even

goat cheese for the burgers, at least not the last time I was there. The rest of the *carte du* goat is pure diner. Aside from a burger, you can get a decent plate of Polish sausage or a tasty sandwich. Even though the BG winds up on many tourists' itineraries, don't let that get your goat, it's still beloved by Chicagoans.

THE BILLY GOAT TAVERN/430 N. MICHIGAN
    AVENUE/ LOWER LEVEL/ TEL: 312-222-1525
Inexpensive

ALINEA – #69

When I first visited Alinea, about four years ago, the buzz about it was intriguing, to say the least. It was said to be in a class by itself. Foodies from everywhere were converging to take a look, as well as a taste. They came away properly dazzled, and so did I, by the creativity and artistic presentation that is so central to Alinea. Its chef, Grant Achatz, seemed a shoo-in to wear the mantle of Charlie Trotter one day. Before opening Alinea, Achatz had cooked under the direction of Thomas Keller at the French Laundry. What a pedigree!

In a short time, Michelin stars began to fall from the heavens onto Grant Achatz's doorstep.

But unfortunately, all the stars and the accolades couldn't keep him from developing cancer of the tongue, a particularly cruel turn of fate for someone who depends on tasting for his life's work. Achatz went through both chemotherapy and radiation which further deadened his taste buds. Through all the pain and depression, he never lost his love for cooking and, most important, his drive to stay a great chef.

Photo by Lara Kastner, courtesy of Alineabook.com

Not only did he recover, but in 2008 Grant Achatz won the James Beard award (I was at the ceremony and there wasn't a dry eye in the house) for the best restaurant in the United States. An even more important reward after all his suffering is that his taste buds have almost returned to normal.

Alinea is tucked into a residential block in a very undistinguished building that looks more like a factory than the home of a posh restaurant. Once you're inside, its exterior is forgotten and the focus is squarely on the food. It's by design

Chef Grant Achatz

that there are no windows—they might distract from the endless array of plates brought to the table. And endless is no exaggeration. For Alinea's most dedicated (not to mention affluent), diners, the 23 (that's not a typo) courses may take almost as long to serve as a change of season. The bill is upwards of $300 per head.

The creations themselves are presented as edible works of art, almost sculptural in design. A transparency of raspberry, yoghurt and rose petals is made to resemble stained glass. A single grape, still attached to its stem, is dressed with a thick coat of peanut butter and chocolate and then wrapped in a delicate shell of brioche dough. Shrimp are threaded onto sticks and then woven together to form an intricate design. To further enhance the drama of it all, the elements of each dish are recited slowly and reverently by dedicated staff. To sum up, Alinea is the kind of place I could write a three act comedy about if I weren't so hopelessly impressed.

ALINEA/ 1723 NORTH HALSTEAD/LINCOLN
   PARK/ TEL: 312- 867-0110
Crushingly Expensive

ALINEA'S MILIEU

Alinea is in a mostly residential area but if you want to house hunt in Chicago, Lincoln Park is a possibility. Failing that, if you happen to be at Alinea for lunch, it's only a short cab ride to the Chicago History Museum.

DRAKE HOTEL'S DICKENS BUFFET – #70

One of the fondest memories I have of Chicago is of a snowy day with Michigan Avenue lit up by a million tiny lights right before Christmas. I was on my way to the Drake Hotel for its annual Dickens Buffet Lunch.

Perhaps Dickens himself didn't attend, but I'm sure that if he were still around he'd have been there. The Drake's Dickens Buffet is a magnet for all the Tiny Tims around town. Not being tiny and certainly not named Tim, I still found myself enjoying it almost as much.

The long buffet table in the center of the room is laden with enough goodies to make even Oliver Twist say, "No more, Sir." The buffet is a 19th-century English Christmas feast, complete with roast goose, plum pudding and trifle. Trumpeters in full regalia march around the room blowing their holiday hearts out. They herald the arrival

of a boar's head (a medieval note), the yule log and finally, St. Nicholas, who just happens to be in the neighborhood. Even Scrooge would be compelled (grudgingly) to join in the fun. If I'm lucky enough to be in Chicago for the holidays, you can guess that I'll be having lunch with Dickens.

DRAKE HOTEL/ 140 EAST
WALTON PLACE/ TEL:
312-787-2200/
LUNCH/MONTH OF
DECEMBER

🎈 THE DRAKE HOTEL'S MILIEU

Since The Drake Hotel is one of Chicago's lovely landmarks, why not take the time to explore the elegant public rooms of this hotel? There is usually an exhibit or two about the Drake's history. Over the years, almost everyone of note has stayed at the Drake, from Emperor Hirohito to Winston Churchill to Princess Diana. If you decide to skip the Christmas buffet or are in town at another season, the Drake's Cape Cod room has some of the best crab cakes outside Baltimore's city limits.

Empanadas de Puerco

FRONTERA GRILL – #71

If this is Chicago, you may well ask, why would anyone be drinking tequila and eating tacos? Maybe it's because they're lucky enough to be at Frontera Grill, Rick Bayless's casa away from casa.

As a young chef from Oklahoma, Bayless moved to Mexico and then in 1987 arrived in Chicago bringing with him his own dynamite style of Mexican cooking. *Ole!* In a city usually preoccupied with steak and Polish sausages, Bayless's south-of-the-boarder sensibilities made for a new and never ending fiesta.

Rick Bayless has, over the years, made a stunning career in Chicago, wowing the locals with his holy molé made with red peanuts, his heavenly goat cheese stuffed empanadas and his ethereal chipotle glazed sea scallops. Did I mention the steady flow of Topolo margaritas? People line up for hours to get into Rick's and I don't mean the one in Casablanca. It's almost like a land grab to snag one of the rough hewn tables in this Technicolor restaurant, covered with Mexican folk art. The service is topnotch, and since Rick takes the whole staff to Mexico once a year, they are walking encyclopedias of Mexican cuisine.

If there was ever a place to kick back and relax it's here at the Grill. The reason for all the fuss about Frontera, aside from the splendid food, has to do with Rick Bayless himself. One of the best known chefs in Chicago he also manages to be just about everywhere. He's made a successful second career on TV, not to mention his Mexican cookbooks that line the shelves of most Chicago bookstores. You could say that as a chef, Bayless blows *muy caliente* in the Windy City.

chef Rick Bayless

THE FRONTERA GRILL/ 445 N. CLARK
STREET/ TEL: 312-661-1434
Moderate

 THE FRONTERA GRILL'S MILIEU

Up the road at 2122 N. Clark Street you'll find the site of the St. Valentine's Day Massacre. If you strain really hard you might still make out the rat-ta-tat-tat of the machine guns, or at least that's what some of the locals would have you believe although the bloody building no longer exists.

LOU MITCHELL'S – #72

We all know that breakfast is the most marvelous meal of the day. I'll even go one step further and admit that I love breakfast for lunch and dinner as well. Lou Mitchell must agree with me because

he's made an art out of loading a.m. calories onto your plate even before the sun rises (Lou's doors open at 5:30—5:30 a.m., that is. Think 1940s beige plastic booths and green plastic plants.

Not too appealing, you may say. Well, just try to get in on the weekend when Lou Mitchell runs a close second to (or tops attendance at) many of Chicago's houses of worship. At Lou's, it's all about thick toast dripping with melted butter, banana pancakes the size of hub caps, and apple and cheddar omelets that take up half the table. Chickens all over Chicago have given their lives to keep Lou supplied with eggs.

If you're watching your weight, you can be sure that Lou isn't. His menu continues with homemade cinnamon toast, awash in butter and marmalade or, for the more adventurous, a Belgium malted waffle. Eggs with skirt steak, hash browns and feta on toast is considered by the staff to be one of the lighter possibilities. A word to the wise: never go to Lou's before your annual physical. Just crossing the threshold can add five or ten pounds of pure cholesterol.

By now you must have guessed that for me Lou's is heaven on earth or in Chicago to be precise. As far as I know, none of Lou Mitchell's patrons have actually gone into cardiac arrest immediately after leaving, although you never can tell. Anything is possible after breakfast at Lou's, except fitting into your new jeans.

Lou Mitchell's/ 565 W Jackson Blvd./ Tel: 312-939-3111/ opens at 5:30am
Moderate

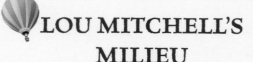

LOU MITCHELL'S MILIEU

Harpo Studios is in the vicinity and if you're in luck you can score some tickets to watch Oprah do her thing (if you're reading this before the summer of 2011), or to hear Dr. Phil give advice. For further info, just call the studio.

Tel: 312- 633-1000/ 1058 W. Washington Blvd.

Chicago/
Front Burner

THE PURPLE PIG

As the saying almost goes, "I never saw a purple pig, I never hope to be one . . ." However, in this case I'm not so sure. The newish Purple Pig is the epitome of everything toothsome in swine satisfaction. There are small plates of porcine tidbits such as pig's ear, crispy fried and sliced paper thin; pig's tongue in red wine vinegar and even pig pate' made from the liver. If this sounds like something the big bad wolf dreamed up, think again. Chicagoans are happily pigging out at this place right in the middle of the Magnificent Mile.

THE PURPLE PIG/ 500 N. MICHIGAN AVE./ TEL: 312-464-1744

PRAIRIE FIRE

Sarah Stegner, longtime Chicago super chef, and twice winner of the James Beard Award, has done it again. Her newest endeavor, Prairie Fire, focuses on contemporary American cuisine, as did her other Chicago restaurants. It's located in the Old Powerhouse Building, one of Chicago's treasured landmarks. The Wild Alaskan Cod in Brioche is definitely making waves.

PRAIRIE FIRE/ 215 N. CLINTON STREET/ TEL: 312-382-8300

New York

"At last the Hudson came into view . . ."

—*Jules Verne*

Phileas arrived in New York late on the evening of December 11, just in time to see his ship, The China, steaming off for Liverpool. Once again, Fogg had missed the boat. One might say a pattern of questionable behavior had emerged.

Phileas knew only too well that his hopes of reaching London in time were disappearing, as fast as The China. The next ship to Liverpool would leave in two days, and that would be too late. What to do? What to do?

Phileas aside, most who come to New York can't wait to get *there* and plan to stay a while. The "Big Apple," as New York is affectionately called by its residents, generates more electricity than Hoover Dam, never makes the slightest attempt to be user friendly and is shockingly expensive. Perhaps the best way to understand New York is to try to understand, no matter how difficult, New Yorkers. The typical New Yorker is Chinese, African-American, Korean, Pakistani, Russian, German, Polish; Muslim, Jewish, Protestant.

Many are a mix of a few ethnic and religious ingredients that have been tossed into its melting pot.

A *real* New Yorker is impossible to define. Like the unicorn, there simply is no such creature.

But being from New York means never having to say, "I don't know." Everybody seems to know everything about everything: where to get the best hotdog in town; where to get the cheapest hotdog in town; where to find a place that still makes egg creams (a rare New York City champagne); what movie theater has the best sound system; what vintage clothing store has the most designer originals. In New York, all is being constantly revealed, like it or not. The name of this strange, native affliction is called, "New York attitude."

The first European visitors, the Dutch, were not seeking political refuge or religious freedom, but rather a northern passage to India as they sailed into New York harbor. When they looked through their spy glasses they saw not just a beautiful coastline but a group of curious beavers looking back at them. The Dutch sailors all had the same response: *furs.* At that very moment, the quest for money and power in New York was born.

After the tragedy of September 11, what New Yorkers used to call "moxie" was the prescription that the city relied on to keep its wounded heart and soul together. That unbelievably sad September day, a day that started out with a blue sky and a bright sun, will never be forgotten by the city. But as any New Yorker will tell you, when the chips are down, "New York, it's a wonderful town." And so it is.

There is a banquet of must-sees in New York, not only for the visitor but also for the poor souls who live here as I do. As soon as I think that I've finally covered all the new sights and read all the new guides, along comes SoHo (south of Houston Street) and then NoHo (north of Houston) and now FiDi (the financial district).

Rome is the Eternal City; London is the capital of what used to be; Paris is dedicated to the intellect and other intangibles. New York is the city of *now!* Tomorrow takes patience and New Yorkers are just too eager to wait.

Eating out in New York is a favorite pastime, a citywide passion. New Yorkers consider their town itself the eating capital of the world although there are some that might dispute that somewhat chauvinistic claim. It's indisputable, however, that New York has more than 25,000 restaurants, representing virtually every cuisine to be found on the globe.

The Pearl Room

FOUR SEASONS – #73

Restaurants come and go in New York faster than a speeding bullet. Some of them are more powerful than a locomotive, and the reputations of their hot celeb chefs can leap to the top of the heap in a single bound. But my favorites tend to be the ones that have been aged like fine wine and are burnished a bit by time. They are my personal hall-of-famers, and heading my list is the Four Seasons.

I suppose if you put a gun to my head and demanded that I tell you where I would go if I could have only one iconic meal in New York, I would have to say, Four Seasons. Not because the food is as exquisite as it is at Jean Georges or as classic as it is at Daniel or as intellectual as the offerings at Ducasse. It's because the Four Seasons is simply the most ravishing restaurant in New York.

Almost a half century ago, it was opened to be *le dernier cri* of modernism. Little has changed. Housed in a Mies van der Rohe's landmarked building (Seagram Building), the restaurant itself was designed by Philip Johnson. Some say that Johnson agreed to do it because he couldn't find a really great-looking place to have lunch, so he created one. Even today, it continues to exude

Chain curtains
Facing page: Le Tricorne *by Picasso*

a cutting edge sensibility. The Four Seasons is simply timeless.

When I first climbed the staircase to the Grill Room, I was not only astonished but dwarfed by the heroic use of space. The sheer drama of 20-foot high ceilings and floor-to-ceiling windows is nothing if not breathtaking. The windows are curtained with long rows of slender chains in constant motion as they catch the breeze.

The Grill Room means, in more ways than one, business. At lunch you can almost smell the smoke of big deals being ignited. It (figuratively) hangs over the tables of the city's top publishers and CEOs as they negotiate massive amounts of money, not to mention prestige, while casually nibbling

on the crudités that are always served. Food is clearly not the only thing on the menu. And when it's ordered in the Grill Room, at least, it's usually served raw. Steak tartare, oysters on the half shell or smoked salmon festooned with caviar, each a perfect choice for a predator.

But make no mistake, the Four Seasons has its romantic side. To find it you'll be ushered through the cavernous, travertine-lined foyer, more like a museum than a restaurant, with Picasso's huge tapestry, *Le Tricorne*, gracing one of its walls. Originally the artist created it as a theater curtain. The effect is awesome. The majestic Pool Room, which runs the gamut from lavish to sumptuous, is bound to elicit oohs and ahs. Full grown trees at each corner of the white marble reflecting pool give the space the look of a terrace. The trees as well as the décor change with the season (remember the name of the place) and the tables are placed wide apart for the ultimate restaurant luxury: space.

The menu in the Pool Room is vaguely continental and focuses on grills and roasts which are brought to the table in festive presentations. If you have a sweet tooth and a little luck, Duck in Orange may be one of your choices. And, there is always a bowl filled with the tiny, buttery croissants, a dangerous distraction while waiting.

A word about dessert, actually two: Chocolate Velvet. To be absolutely precise: "Four Season's Chocolate Velvet." The Four Seasons has been serving its Chocolate Velvet since 1959, and so it has delighted generations.

Once you stop comparing the Four Seasons' kitchen to the culinary cathedrals of France, you can just sit back and savor its luxe approach to the good life.

THE FOUR SEASONS/99 EAST 52ND STREET/
   TEL: 212-754-9494
Very Expensive

FOUR SEASON'S MILIEU

Walk west to Fifth Avenue and turn downtown to take a look at New York's answer to Notre Dame: St. Patrick's Cathedral in all its gothic-style grandeur. It's an antidote to the secular power and glory of the Four Seasons. Across the street from St. Pat's is Saks Fifth Avenue and you're back to glory and power. After all, you're in New York, not Frozen Sneaker, Nebraska.

CARNEGIE DELI – #74

Just let your imagination run wild for a moment. Where would Broadway Danny Rose meet the Prince of Wales for dinner? At the Carnegie Deli, of course.

If anyone asked me what kind of food was the most authentic and indicative of the New York I grew up in, I would have to say, "delicatessen." Hundreds of years ago, when I was taken out to dinner by my parents, it wasn't to a chic little French bistro, it was to a delicatessen. And that in no way translates into the deli of today. No hero sandwiches, no ham on whole-wheat and definitely no tuna torpedoes. The menu I was handed in my very first delicatessen featured pastrami or corned beef on rye, the sustenance of choice for the Ashkenazi Jews who immigrated to New York in the 1800s and 1900s, accompanied by sour pickles. In fact, bowls of sour pickles were placed on every table as if they were floral arrangements.

(At the Carnegie Deli, they still are.)

Some of the more adventurous diners dared to order chopped liver and the really brave asked for tongue on rye, though that was thought to be a very bold choice, indeed. Back then, almost every neighborhood had its own delicatessen. The delicatessens were part of the fabric of the city.

courtesy of Caragie Deli

Corned Beef Sandwich

One by one they started to disappear as the threat of open heart surgery became just too loud to ignore.

Today the Carnegie Deli is known by people all over the world because of its excellence. Many New Yorkers value it as an endangered species. Years ago the owner tried to open a branch in Los Angeles and failed miserably, much to the disappointment of ex-pats from New York. It had something to do with the water used to steam the meat. It just wasn't New York water, and the pastrami and corned beef went on strike.

Part of the Carnegie's charm is its total lack of charm. The noise and the blindingly bright lights create the ambiance of a hospital Emergency Room on a Saturday night. The waiters assume that you don't know what the hell you're ordering and insist you just leave it to them. Even when you know, it's easier to just leave it to them. No matter how strange the whole process may seem to you, that is if you're a civilized person, the

sandwiches are spectacular as well as gargantuan. The chicken soup comes with a matzo ball the size of Jupiter. And the cheesecake, don't ask! The best advice I can give you about how to approach the Carnegie is just to go, and leave it to them.

CARNEGIE DELI/ 854 7ᵀᴴ AVENUE/ TEL: 212-757-2245
Moderate

 CARNEGIE DELI'S MILIEU

It's just a block or so from Carnegie Hall (no, the hall wasn't named after the deli; it was the other way around), so you can check out the schedule and plan on attending a future concert. Alternatively, you can walk from the Carnegie down Seventh Avenue to Times Square in about 15 minutes. Or, if the pastrami has put you in a romantic mood, you're even closer to Central Park South (West 59ᵗʰ Street) where you can hail a hansom cab.

---

21 CLUB – #75

The first time I entered the hallowed hallway of "21" it was to meet with an editor after a book contract had been signed. "21" was a favorite place for editors to consummate such agreements with a tribal rite called "the publishing lunch." For years I had been passing those statues of brightly colored jockeys that line the clubby restaurant's

outside steps, beckoning me to come in and be a good sport. However, being a good sport at "21" could means signing over half of your 401K, and so for me the safest option had been to just keep on going.

What struck me as I waited for my Prince of Paperbacks was that there wasn't a table in sight,

continued on page 234

Photo by Battman NYC, Courtesy of '21'

Profiteroles at 21

just a few comfortable chairs to rest in while your bloodline was checked.

Once inside the dining room, it's as though you've wandered onto the set of Lifestyles of the Rich and Hungry. Impossibly handsome young men, wearing suits that cost more than my mortgage payment, discuss their brilliant stock manipulations. Elegantly turned out women of a certain age talk about their latest cosmetic surgery as they pick at Cobb salads. And then, suddenly, someone actually looks familiar. My god, it's a movie star. Is this a great place or what?

Back to my first visit: When I was finally led to a table, deceptively covered by a homey checkered tablecloth, I noticed that the ceiling was covered with every conceivable kind of toy: model planes,

tractors, dump trucks, boats, ballet slippers, on and on, sometimes two and three deep. You know that you've arrived when "21" accepts your contribution to its ceiling.

Prohibition was the great idea behind "21" or beating Prohibition to be more exact. The guys with the huge wads of cash, pinkie rings and cauliflower ears needed a place to hang out and pretend not to be drinking. In other words, "21" was a speakeasy. Martinis and bourbon Old Fashioneds were served in coffee cups to fool the flatfoots. After Prohibition was repealed, the 21 Club began serving drinks in glasses and added burgers and fries to its coffee-cup menu. "21" continues to be one of New York's prized possessions.

(continued on page 236)

21's Grilled Black Bass with Asparagus and Lemon and Caper Vinaigrette

For Lemon and Caper Vinaigrette
- 3 ounces extra virgin olive oil
- 2 lemons (squeeze out juice, remove seeds, reserve skin for zest)
- 1 teaspoon lemon zest (use a micro-plane to grate zest off lemons)
- 1 ounce capers, washed and patted dry
- 1 tablespoon micro-chives, sliced thin or cut with scissors
- 1 tablespoon chervil, chopped, without stems

For Asparagus
- 8 pieces jumbo asparagus, peeled and cut down middle
- 1 ounce diced tomato, peeled

For Black Bass
- 2 tablespoons grapeseed oil
- 2-3 whole black bass, scaled, and filleted with skin on
- Sea salt to taste
- 4 sprigs fresh thyme
- 1 pinch piment d'espelette
- 4 lemon wedges
- 4 ounces herb salad (mix of micro herbs or blend of soft herbs such as chervil, tarragon and chives)

SERVES 4

For vinaigrette, in a bowl or airtight container, mix all ingredients together.

Preheat grill or build fire and let charcoal ash over, clean grill grate and wipe down with a touch of grapeseed oil on a rag.

Boil water in a large pot, enough to easily fit the asparagus without the ends sticking out of the pot.

Season bass filets with salt and brush each filet with grapeseed oil.

Place fish on grill, skin side down, place a sprig of fresh thyme on top and cook 4-5 minutes.

Place asparagus into boiling, salted water and cook until just tender, about 3 minutes. Remove and place on warm plates.

Return to the fish, remove thyme and gently turn fish over on the flesh side and grill until just cooked through, about another 2-3 minutes, depending on grill temperature. (You can check the fish with a cake tester by inserting it into the flesh. If the cake tester slides easily into the fish, it's done.)

Remove fish from grill and place on warm plate with asparagus. Drizzle fish with lemon and caper vinaigrette and season with some piment and sea salt.

Garnish with herb salad and lemon wedge.

The fact that food is served at this pit-stop for millionaires is a definite plus but not of great importance. The "21 burger" is what most people order because it's straightforward. Various grilled meat and fish are available along with other choices. The menu is certainly not one of the more creative in town but it's one of the more expensive. Never mind—it's "21," and tables are as filled as its ceilings. Most of its patrons just think of the tab as an admission charge to one of the best shows in town.

21 CLUB'S MILIEU

I think that there is simply no other option during the day but to walk around the corner to the Museum of Modern Art (MOMA) at 11 West 53rd. If you resist expanding your knowledge of Modernism then there is always non-stop shopping at MOMA's gift shops or up and down Fifth Avenue.

21 Club/ 21 West 52 Street/
Tel: 212-582-7200
Painfully Expensive

THE GOTHAM BAR AND GRILL – #76

The Gotham is guaranteed to raise your artistic consciousness as well as your culinary expectations as soon as you walk through the door. The chic restaurant boasts architectural innovation and an art collection impressive enough to have its own curator. Platforms of various levels and angles divide the former warehouse's generous space and snoods of parachute cloth float around the chandeliers like white clouds. Tall windows make the room seem almost baronial. Gotham's visual drama seems to generate an electricity in its eclectic clientele. It's been said that at Gotham, diners wearing denim are as comfortable as those sporting the latest Armani.

Owner-chef Alfred Portale who started Gotham in 1985 was in his pre-gastronomic days a jewelry designer. He devised Gotham's menu to present diners with his distinctive take on American cuisine. No painted plates for Portale; his selections arrive at the table in 3D splendor. Sculptural towers of salad and gemlike mosaics of seafood are among his designs. Portale once told

me "food should be clever but delicious." Through the years he has more than kept his word.

When I last visited Gotham, I couldn't resist the seafood salad—a spiral of crusty crustaceans headed for the ceiling. The extravagant salads include heirloom tomatoes and are also quite literally upwardly mobile. The perfectly done miso-marinated cod is served snoozing under a blanket of manila clams. For dessert, Gotham's chocolate cake is legendary but the Blood Orange Soufflé, served with mango jam and caramelized phyllo, is another showstopper. Decisions, decisions!

GOTHAM BAR AND GRILL / 12 EAST 12TH STREET/ TEL: 212-620-4020
Expensive

GOTHAM BAR AND GRILL'S MILIEU

The Gotham is just steps away from some wonderful "nabes." Stroll west for a minute or two and you'll be on lower Fifth Avenue. Look left and behold Washington Square Park with its copy of the Arc de Triomphe. *Follow the vision into the center of Greenwich Village. Or if you go east on 12th street after leaving the restaurant and then head down to 8th Street you'll be in the East Village, within walking distance of the Public Theater on Lafayette.*

BUBBY'S – #77

There are many choices for breakfast or shall we say, brunch in the city but my favorite, bagels down, is Bubby's. It opened its doors in 1990, an eternity ago for New York. Some would now call it a venerable institution. It started with only two tables in a gritty manufacturing area of the city's west side, south of even grittier Canal Street. And then, before you could say "gentrify," the neighborhood was renamed Tribeca (Triangle below Canal) and became one of the city's trendiest. Bubby's woke up one morning to find it had become a goldmine: apartments across the

(continued on page 241)

street were selling for 2.5 million—dollars, that is.

Bubby's formal name is Bubby's Pie Company, and true to that description, there are over 10 different kinds of house-made pie on the menu daily. Bubby's churns its own ice cream, smokes its own salmon and even makes its own soda, using only pure cane sugar, not that corn syrup stuff. Its motto is: "We buy it only if we can't make it ourselves, better." The moral of the story: Don't fool around with Bubby. And that goes double for reservations. There are none.

Breakfast at Bubby's can have the same effect as an affair of the heart: the memory lingers on. Grits smothered in cheese, steel-cut oatmeal swimming in butter and heavy cream, plates of bacon and eggs heaped with hash browns and, of course, pie, pie and more pie. If you're on the South Beach Diet, you're going to have a really hard time.

Bubby's is as cozy and down home as having breakfast in your own Bubby's (grandmother's) kitchen. Do you remember how happy it made her to watch you eat? As Yogi Berra said, "It's like déjà vu all over again."

BUBBY'S/120 HUDSON STREET/ TEL: 212- 219- 0666- NO RESERVATIONS
Moderate

 BUBBY'S MILIEU

From Tribeca it's a do-able walk down Broadway to Ground Zero which is likely to still be a construction site. From there, the FiDi is at your feet. Bowling Green Park at the tip of Broadway is right next to the giant bronze bull, the symbol of Wall Street. He may or may not be a sight for sore losers, depending on the market. You might decide to just walk over to the New York Stock Exchange and throw stones. If you walk uptown from Bubby's you'll soon come to SoHo where there is still some art along with a lot of upscale merchandise. After all that pie at Bubby's, any kind of walk would be a blessing.

THE UNION SQUARE CAFÉ – #78

Where to find a comfortable, friendly place for the moderately affluent or the soon to be extremely rich and famous? The Union Square Café fills that bill. I'll have to admit right from the get go that I love Danny Meyer, one of New York's most respected restaurateurs. The restaurant community in New York has been known to occasionally singe its asparagus over some supposed infraction, such as "thou shalt not freeze" or another culinary taboo. But whenever Danny is mentioned, complaint seems absent. I have never heard anything but admiration for his ever growing restaurant realm or his many charitable works. And then there's the fact that Danny Meyer bears a more than passing resemblance to Jerry Seinfeld. As to that, I can only point out that they've never been seen together, so draw your own conclusion.

When Union Square Café opened in '85 it was considered to be a yuppie "21." Then Publisher's Row moved down from midtown to Union Square, and brought a new scene to the café. Lunch is the time to see and be seen if you are a writer or an editor. The room buzzes with gossipy tidbits about foreign rights or bestseller lists or the word that makes a writer's heart beat faster: advance. You might have need of a super computer just to tally up the collective SAT scores at the tables, and not only at lunch. Business continues to be serious business even during the dinner hour.

Since Danny created Union Square Café, his culinary brood has increased to include many new restaurants around town that are all wonderful, each in its own special way, but for me the Union Square Café is still cooking on all burners.

Risotto

The café's main room, with its bare, highly polished wooden floor and generously spaced tables, isn't just concerned with book clubs and bond futures, or even just plain futures, it's about sheep's milk cheese ravioli with black peppercorns or the caramelized onion risotto or the crisp fried calamari with anchovy mayonnaise. Recognizable, delicious food is the order of the day here. I've often seen Danny going from table to table, shaking hands and giving tips on the wine list but you have to catch him on the fly. He has a mini-empire to guide, and he does it with great flare.

Raviolini

UNION SQUARE CAFÉ/ 21 EAST 16ᵀᴴ STREET/
TEL: 212-243-4020
Expensive

 UNION SQUARE'S MILIEU

You're just steps away from the Union Square Green Market. It's the closest New York has come to some of those great European food markets, even though it's a rather pale version, The market is open Monday, Wednesday, Friday and Saturday from 8 a.m.-6 p.m. Or if you're in the mood for some very expensive shopping or looking, then stroll east to ABC Carpet & Home on Broadway. Not just devoted to rugs, as its name implies, it has an international array of furniture and home accessories, including antiques and exotic craftworks from around the world.

GRAY'S PAPAYA – #79

Street food in New York is multicultural in the same way that the city is. Each area has its own particular kind of nosh to eat as you go. You name the kind of food, and you can find it on some cart or a small aluminum truck with a vendor who frequently speaks only Mandarin or Urdu. But there's also a type of street food that's not exactly on the street. It's really a storefront with a counter. The best of the lot is Gray's Papaya.

There are several around the city but Gray's on

the Upper West Side seems the most dedicated to serving a dog that's really "hot." The quality is as good as it can get for an object that's stuffed with a blend of mystery meat and overwhelmed with sautéed onions, relish and sauerkraut. Gray's swears on a stack of buns that its frank is definitely 100% pure beef, and sometimes you just have to relax, accept and enjoy. The hordes of people who jam the place at all hours seem willing to take Gray's at its word, but after the Bush administration, who knows?

The accompanying liquid refreshment at Gray's is either a glass of the ever popular Papaya drink

or in my case, a "flute" of coconut champagne, non vintage, of course. This has to be one of the cheapest, most satisfying snacks in town.

GRAY'S PAPAYA/ 2090 BROADWAY AT 72ND STREET/ TEL: DON'T EVEN THINK ABOUT IT
Super Cheap

IL MULINO – #80

If the very fictional Tony Soprano begin to pine for the very fictional Carmela's homemade manicotti after a hard day doing don't-ask-what in Manhattan, where would he tell his driver to take him? My guess is Il Mulino.

The brothers, Fernando and Gino Masci who opened Il Mulino in 1981, were born in the Abruzzi region of Italy and for them home is where the cannelloni and the fusilli wear their *pomodoro* sauce with pride. The Abruzzi is in southern Italy near Rome, and its food is known for rustic, simple combinations of meats, pastas

and sauces, liberally flavored with garlic. Il Mulino follows that foolproof recipe for success with its homemade pastas and even homier sausages.

Ever since it opened, Il Mulino has attracted the *vitello parmigiano* set from all over the globe. Italian comfort food is getting harder and harder to come by since a new dedication to Milanese cuisine has been spreading faster than gossip at the hairdressers. Fortunately, for those who continue to love the golden oldies of southern Italian cooking, in the world according to Il Mulino, *nuovo Italiano* is simply unheard of.

However, food is not the whole story at Il Mulino. Even though its surroundings are small, cramped and decidedly unglamorous, this is no ordinary neighborhood Italian restaurant. Just try getting a reservation. It's almost impossible unless you've been coming for years and have added gazillions of dollars to Il Mulino's coffers, not including the tip. And if all that were not enough, two Presidents of The United States of America, Bill Clinton and Barack Obama, decided to meet there for lunch. Could things get any worse?

If you finally land one of Il Mulino's coveted reservations, things will get significantly better. Immediately upon being seated, multiple platters heaped with crisp breaded zucchini, garlic

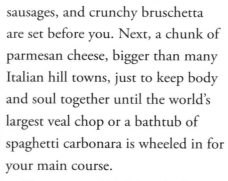

sausages, and crunchy bruschetta are set before you. Next, a chunk of parmesan cheese, bigger than many Italian hill towns, just to keep body and soul together until the world's largest veal chop or a bathtub of spaghetti carbonara is wheeled in for your main course.

The menu at Il Mulino looks pretty much the same as it did when I first visited in the '80s. The one addition I've noticed was the Risotto alla Milanese, but I think that's just on the menu as a front in case someone from Michelin stops

IL MULINO'S MILIEU

Il Mulino is in the very heart of Greenwich Village, at one time New York's answer to Paris' left bank. In the '20s and '30s, artists such as Eugene O'Neill, Isadora Duncan and William Faulkner were drawn to the coffee houses that lined its streets. Caffé Reggio and the Caffé Dante are still there. MacDougal Street is the address for both, just a short distance from Il Mulino. A perfect postscript to your meal would be a perfect espresso.

by. A far more nostalgic choice is the raviolini stuffed with veal, lamb, beef or spinach. Desserts are for those with really good medical insurance. A napoleon that would bring tears to the eyes of the Short One, a silky panna cotta (Italian crème brulée) that lingers on the tongue and, last but not least, an after-dinner glass of 100 proof grappa, on the house.

It's true that even with a reservation you'll wait for a table at Il Mulino, the place can be noisy, the prices seem like quotes from the national debt and the service is slow.

The grappa always makes me dizzy but I don't really care, I just love the place.

Il Mulino- 86 West 3ʳᵈ Street/
Tel: 212- 673-3783

New York City/
Front Burner

CORTON

When Drew Nieporent opens a new restaurant, New Yorkers stop to take careful notice. Not only that, they run to their phones to make reservations. They know from grim experience that their chances of actually getting one are slim to nothing unless they choose to have dinner at 2 a.m.

Named after a wine region in France, Corton has replaced Nieporent's brilliant Montrachet, long an elegant outpost for Tribeca' serious foodies. You could say that Corton is to the manor born.

CORTON/ 239 WEST BROADWAY/
TEL: 212-219-2777

SHANG

Most of what's new in Manhattan restaurants happens to be going on in one of the oldest parts of the city, the Lower East Side. It has become gourmet central in part because its relatively cheap rents attract the latest migrant chefs. Shang, one of the best of the new restaurants, is run by a super-chef from north-of-the-border, Toronto.

The menu is devoted to Asian-Fusion. Shang's surroundings may not give the Four Seasons much to worry about but what's on the plate is picture perfect.

SHANG /187 ORCHARD STREET/ THOMPSON
HOTEL/ TEL: 212-260-7900

~Phileas Fogg's Return~
LONDON, AT LAST!

Phileas Fogg disembarked in the British Isles at 11:40 a.m. on what he counted as the 80th day of his journey, ready to marry Aouda, and whisk his himself to the Reform Club before he lost his bet.

But detective Fixx was at the end of the dock. Game change: Fixx arrested Fogg and dragged him off to jail.

After a night in jail, proof emerged that Phileas had not robbed a bank before leaving England. He was released in the morning; it was too late!

Or was it? Phileas Fogg, who always knew the hour and minute didn't know what day it was. He had failed to calculate the day gained for crossing the International Date Line while steaming across the Pacific Ocean.

The whist players, whom Fogg had left 80 days earlier, rose to their feet in disbelief as he strode through the front door of the Reform Club. "Here I am gentlemen," Phileas calmly announced, with three seconds to spare at 8:44 p.m. on December 21, 1872.

Time and tide wait for no man, but Phileas Fogg may have been a really impressive exception.

Phileas Fogg's journey is at an end and so is mine. We both went around the world, he in 80 days and I in 80 meals. We both had some marvelous escapades. Which one of us had the most fun?

You decide.

—*Nan Lyons*

EPILOGUE

The Reform Club sits solidly in Pall Mall separated by St. James Park from the houses of Parliament. It was a relatively new club when Jules Verne (who had never visited it) picked it as the scene setter for his novel.

The club had opened in 1836 as a haven for members of the Reform party, gentlemen who had supported the 1832 Reform Act which had extended the right to vote to a small group of Englishmen. The other radical idea club founders seem to have had was using food as a membership builder. The club snagged Alexis Soyer, the top French chef in London, as its cook.

Eventually, the club became a magnet for literary men. Its rolls included William Thackeray, Arthur Conan Doyle, Henry James and H.G. Wells. Winston Churchill also belonged. The radicalism of the Reform Club went just so far. It wasn't until 1981 that a woman could unwind in the club. Today, more than half the members are female. What would Phileas have thought of that?

Its menu has changed but not entirely. Terence Howard presides over the kitchen these days. A native Londoner, he whisked and sautéed at the Savoy before transferring his elegant touch to a clubbier atmosphere. There have been several nods to contemporary tastes, such as Caesar Salad and Scallops with Linguini, but the menu still supports a cart of roasted meats and at least one retro pudding for dessert.

Soyer, the first celebrity chef, was the creator of the lamb chop dish that became the club's signature entrée: Reform Cutlets. The recipes for this and other oldies but goodies on today's menu, follow.

THE REFORM CLUB/ 104 PALL MALL/ LONDON/ MEMBERS ONLY

The Kitchen Department of the Reform Club *by John Tarring, 1842*

 Chicken Consommé

This Reform Club consommé is a respectable chicken vegetable soup rather than a clear broth

- *4 chicken legs*
- *1 medium white onion, peeled and chopped*
- *2 celery stalks, washed and chopped*
- *1 leek, cleaned, white and light green part, chopped*
- *2 cloves garlic, peeled and minced*
- *3 bay leaves*
- *5 peppercorns*
- *2 sprigs rosemary*
- *3 sprigs thyme*
- *1 medium carrot, chopped*
- *2 large egg whites*
- *2 ounces unsalted butter*
- *Truffle oil to taste*
- *Chopped chives*
- *Salt and pepper to taste*

YIELDS 4 CUPS

Roughly chop ¾ of the onion, celery, carrot and leek, reserving ¼ of the amount of each. Roughly chop the rosemary and thyme. Melt the butter in a heavy-bottomed pan; add the vegetable, herbs, garlic, chicken, peppercorns and bay leaves. Cook over low heat until the onions are soft, approximately 10 minutes stirring occasionally. Add enough water to cover the vegetables and chicken (about 4 cups), bring to a boil, then simmer for 1½ hours. Remove the chicken legs and pick off meat.

Mince the remaining onion, leek, celery and carrot, lightly beat the egg whites and fold in the vegetables to bind them all together. Bring the consommé back to the boil and add the egg white mixture, gently stir in to create a raft, reduce the heat to a gentle simmer. Continue to simmer for 1 hour. Make a hole at one edge of the pot and carefully pass off the liquor through a cheese cloth into another pot. Add the chicken, chopped chives, truffle oil and salt and pepper to taste.

You may want to refrigerate the soup overnight so that you may scrape off the fat before heating and serving.

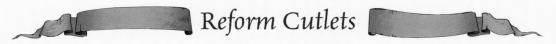

Reform Cutlets

- 8 (French-cut) lamb chops
- 3 ounces ham
- 1¾ ounces tongue
- 1¾ ounces cooked beet
- 1 ounce gherkin-pickles
- 2 eggs
- 2 ounces breadcrumbs

For the Sauce
- 10 tablespoons lamb [or beef] stock
- 1 teaspoon tomato puree [paste]
- 2½ tablespoons Tarragon or white-wine vinegar
- 3½ tablespoons red wine
- 2 tablespoons red currant jelly
- 2 peppercorns
- 1 shallot
- 2 garlic cloves
- 1oz butter

Separate egg whites from yolks. Place egg whites on Saran wrap and steam over boiling water until firm. Refrigerate the whites.

Chop finely one-third of the ham and mix with breadcrumbs.

Cut the rest of the ham, the tongue, gherkin, and firm egg white into batons [thin strips]. Set aside.

Season lamb chops with salt and pepper, brush with egg yolk and press on the breadcrumbs.

Place chops in a frying pan over low heat. Fry chops on one side for approximately two-minutes then turn over for another two. Each side should be golden brown.

For the sauce, finely chop garlic and shallot. Melt butter in a pan, add garlic and shallot, stirring for 1 minute.

Add tomato paste and stir for another minute.

Add vinegar, wine and peppercorns and stir until liquid is reduced by about a third.

Add stock and currant jelly and reduce sauce by a half.

Add meat, egg-white and pickle batons to sauce, allow them to heat through briefly and place in a sauce boat. Serve with hot lamp chops.

Alternately, place batons in a serving dish, cover with heated sauce and place lamb chops on top. Serve immediately.

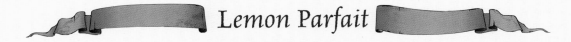

Lemon Parfait

Whisk 1⅛ cup of superfine sugar and pasteurized egg yolk (the equivalent of 6 raw yolks) until the mixture is light and creamy, then add 1½ ounces of lemon juice to the mix.

Stiffly whisk 2 cups of cream then gently fold into mix, fill individual ramekins, freeze for approximately 3 hours then serve.

*Recipes are courtesy of Terence Howard, chief chef of the Reform Club. The Chicken Consommé recipe was adapted by Cooking by the Book, New York, NY. The Reform Cutlet recipe was adapted by chef Gary Rhodes for the October 2009 issue of BBC's Inside Out.

ACKNOWLEDGMENTS

The author wishes to thank Samantha Lyons who, as the daughter of a writer, has known all the pain that comes with the birth of a book and none of the pleasures; Paul Tunis who, as an editor extraordinaire, has exhibited the compassion of a Buddhist monk and the endless patience of a kindergarten teacher; and Janet Rodgers who believes that travel has far more nutritional value than broccoli. Last but certainly not least, I wish to thank both Ian Kenworthy, house manager of the Reform Club in London, and Terry Howard, the club's head chef, for invaluable assistance in helping me create a possible dinner menu for Phileas Fogg from a *carte de jour* of his period. They were also kind enough to contribute recipes.

—*N. L.*

INDEX

~ABOUT THE AUTHOR~

NAN LYONS is one of America's treasured food and travel writers.

She and her late-husband Ivan Lyons wrote several notable novels, including *Someone Is Killing the Great Chefs of Europe,* followed by the script for the worldwide hit movie, *Who Is Killing the Great Chefs of Europe?* They also wrote a sequel, *Someone Is Killing the Great Chefs of America.*

In recent years, Nan Lyons has contributed to *Bon Appetit* and authored luxury travel guides and the highly-praised *Gluttony: More is More.*